*This book is dedicated to anyone who
has ever felt stuck in between.*

"J. Allen Cross has done an extraordinary job of providing us with a book filled with rich invaluable information about our culture and magical traditions. He has done a superb job of sharing this information with genuine heartfelt authenticity, love, and respect, which makes it an absolutely delightful read! Gracias!"

—Erika Buenaflor, MA, JD, author of
Cleansing Rites of Curanderismo

"J. Allen Cross opens a box of secrets and spells deeply linked to the culture, myth, history, and blood of his ancestors. *American Brujeria* explores folklore as well as history, and guides readers through spells and rituals. Learn how to do a *limpia* in the morning, afternoon, night, or anytime you are drinking your *cafe con leche*."

—Elhoim Leafar, author of *The Magical Art
of Crafting Charm Bags* and *Manifestation Magic*

"A landmark book that blends the living traditions of folk magic, culture, and modern spiritual belief, *American Brujeria* is cross-cultural and deeply impactful. J. Allen Cross has made sure that this work will be accessible to not only this generation but future generations, as well. The magic is potent, raw, and real. Each page had me more excited and energized than the last."

— Temperance Alden, author of *Year of the Witch*

"In *American Brujeria*, J. Allen Cross finds a way to explore the heritage and practices of Mexican folk and spiritual traditions by building on their foundations and making them approachable to American (and beyond) audiences searching for the *magia* (magic) and wisdom of their own culture. We need more authors of color like Cross to illuminate these rich and time-honored practices."

—Alexis A. Arredondo and Eric J. Labrado
of City Alchemist, authors of *Magia Magia*

"A much-needed book, *American Brujeria* serves a community—Mexican Americans—who find themselves trying to find spaces where they fit. It combines aspects of Mexican Brujeria with various American magical influences, including even Puerto Rican Espiritismo. It's a great place to start if you find yourself in this twilight space and need to know where to begin. *American Brujeria* offers a great foundation, as well as various practices that a reader can engage in to begin this wonderful journey. Beautifully written and something any reader is sure to enjoy."

—Hector Salva, author of *The 21 Divisions*

"*American Brujeria* offers a good look into a culture that I feel many folks outside of that culture don't understand. I especially love the part about the only person the devil fears is a grandmother—it makes me think of my mother-in-law who blessed us every night before we went to sleep at her house. *American Brujeria* opens the door for outsiders to look in and to be able to feel the power of Mexican American culture through the works provided here. This is a great book that will help many."

—Starr Casas, author of *Old Style Conjure*

"J. Allen Cross, your book is pure *magick*, and could only have been written by you. I am grateful that you're spreading the knowledge of the magickal part of our ancient culture with respect, honor, and love, and also for reminding us—the people 'in between'—of the strength, charm, power, and pride that is our ancestors' legacy. When I read your book, it produced in me a *limpia* of my soul and reinforced my spirit with passion and courage to keep on spreading our Brujeria. You did a remarkable job researching our ancestral magick. This is a must-have book in the personal library of every serious student of magick."

—Martha Ileana Moran Gonzalez, founder and director of *Witchmart*, high priestess, and proud bruja

"Bravo for *American Brujeria* by J. Allen Cross. This book is a folkloric gem, a magical treasure trove, and a wisdom-window into some of the time-honored practices of Mexican Brujeria, and his own Mexican American Brujeria. Cross is a beacon of cultural competence and respect in this well-written, sincere, insightful, and practical book. It offers historical context, cultural education, applicable and relevant recipes, potent magical and healing workings, and culturally unique lore. To all this, he adds a unique gem indeed—sound ethical advice for interested potential practitioners who are not of Mexican descent on how to honor and respect the tradition, its culture, and the ancestors. Now, open this wisdom-window of a book and see what it will open in *you*."

—Orion Foxwood, author of *Mountain Conjure and Southern Rootwork*

"A treasured volume packed full of magic, and deeply steeped in the history and lore of J. Allen Cross's rich culture, *American Brujeria* is filled with folk stories, saints, and spirits alongside prayers, spells, baths, floor washes, and cleansings. A much-needed and long-awaited guide that is sure to be a foundation for young witches while still providing deep knowledge and practices for advanced practitioners, Cross's dedication to his path and culture comes across beautifully in this book, which is sure to be an instant classic."

—Annwyn Avalon, author of *Water Witchcraft* and *The Way of the Water Priestess*

"*American Brujeria* demystifies Mexican American folk magic and makes it accessible to anyone wanting to get in touch with their magical heritage, as well as those interested in this beautiful magico-religious practice. J. Allen Cross's wonderfully rich book explores the history and bridges the generational and cultural gap between Mexicans and their Mexican American descendants. *American Brujeria* serves as a comprehensive guide for beginners as well as seasoned practitioners wanting to reconnect to their roots. An excellent tribute to this powerful tradition."

—Mary-Grace Fahrun, author of *Italian Folk Magic*

AMERICAN BRUJERIA

★ Modern ★
Mexican American Folk Magic

J. ALLEN CROSS

WEISER
BOOKS

This edition first published in 2021 by Weiser Books, an imprint of
Red Wheel/Weiser, LLC
With offices at:
65 Parker Street, Suite 7
Newburyport, MA 01950
www.redwheelweiser.com

ISBN: 978-1-57863-745-4
Library of Congress Cataloging-in-Publication Data
available upon request.

Cover design by Kathyrn Sky-Peck
Interior by Steve Amarillo / Urban Design LLC
Typeset in Adobe Sabon, Marmelad, and Archer

Printed in the United States of America
IBI
10 9 8 7 6 5 4 3 2 1

Contents

Chapter Four: Las Velas / 59

Chapter Five: Los Santos / 89

Chapter Six: La Muerte / 117

Chapter Seven: Limpias / 127

Chapter Eight: Hechizos / 163

Chapter Nine: Los Antepasados / 203

Acknowledgments

I wish to say thank you to everyone who helped make this book a success . . .

To Raul, Edgar, Ashley, and Jose from Magnolia, your stories helped bring this book to life.

To Rosanna Van Horn, for sharing her family prayers and *hechizos* with me. This book would be much less magical without your beautiful presence.

To Angelica Mitchell, for volunteering your time to help a stranger translate their broken Spanish. May others be inspired by your kindness.

To my mother Christine, for always supporting me and for organizing the interviews behind the scenes. It means more to me than you will ever know.

To my husband Joshua, for his enormous patience and support through this process. You are the best partner I could ask for.

To Annwyn Avalon, for holding my hand through this and urging me to make this dream a reality. You were my rock, and I might not have been brave enough without you.

To Judika Illes, for believing in me and my vision and for helping make this book a reality. You made my dreams come true.

Introduction: Spanglish

The day I pitched this book to my editor, I was struck with the sobering realization that I had a responsibility to do it right. And it was not a responsibility just to myself, but to my community. I owed it to my people—*mi gente*. Immediately, I was overwhelmed with the enormity of the project. As a Mexican person myself, I had experience and knowledge on my side, but I knew this book would be so much bigger than who I am and what I had been taught. I felt unworthy to speak for my community and worried that I would let them down. So what else was there to do? I turned to them. I spoke to everyone with Mexican heritage I could find, starting with friends and moving out to complete strangers. I braced myself for the worst.

As a person whose family has been in the United States for several generations, I worried I would be perceived as an outsider or imposter. But the positive response was overwhelming. My community embraced me with open arms as one of their own. They told me their stories freely, as I scribbled away in my notebook, soaking in every word. Excited about the project, they were eager to tell me everything they knew. When they ran out of things to share, they would call their mothers or bring them to me in person to tell me everything they couldn't. Folks who didn't even know me were happy to sit down and talk to me about the day that *La Virgen* gave them directions when they were running from the police or the day their father saw the monstrous creature *El Cucuy* on the banks of a river. I learned that in Guanajuato, brujas steal the eyes from cats so they can see at night while they fly through the trees. They told me all the uses for red string and that you could banish ghosts by swearing at them profusely. I was taught that an old boot has plenty of uses, including as an aid in astral projection, and that Vicks VapoRub really does cure all. I was humbled and deeply inspired by their stories, their wisdom, and the faith they had—not just in their culture, but in me. This book started out as a project about magic, but truly it's about all of them—their stories and their memories.

It's safe to say this book is for the Mexican people living in America. To all of us who are both *Mexicano* and American, this book is for you. It is a love letter to all of you who have felt your parents' hands on your back, as they pushed you forward in front of strangers because you spoke English, even though you were just a child. This book is for you with the *café con leche* skin and the tongue that can't quite remember that one Spanish word. It's for you, the one who has to live your days hoping that Spanglish will see you through and *La Virgen* will still listen when you pray to her in that same twisted tongue. It's for the victims of assimilation, colonization, and deprivation who have no one left to teach them how to pray *El Padre Nuestro* even though their soul cries out for it. It's for the ones who are several generations American, the ones who come from Mexican families but "don't look Mexican," the ones who are a half or quarter Mexican and don't know what that means for them.

This book is for all who are caught in between—who feel the pull of two different worlds struggling so hard to bring you to one side or the other that you may just split in two. Are you the past, or are you the future? Are you your ancestors, or are you something new? The answer is both. You are *you*, and you exist in between—but you are not alone. You have *gente*. We might not all be "Mexicans from Mexico," and most of us are not even full Mexican. We are, however, valid descendants of the Mexican people. Our ancestors are Mexican, Chicanx, Maya, Aztec, *y más*. We are a people between worlds, and our ancestors of that land are here with us, coursing through our veins and asking us to find *nuestra magia* once more. And we can find it where we stand, right here, in the space between.

It is my hope and intent that anyone who feels disconnected from their Mexican heritage may pick up this book and open up a complete guide to making their way back home. I pray that this book finds its way into the hands of those who have no one left to teach them to pray the rosary and tell them the stories of our people. I hope this book acts as a bridge connecting you to our ancestors and gives you the confidence to walk in their power once more. Here you will learn how to work with candles, saints, herbs, and more! By reclaiming our ancestral magic, we can soothe the wounds of colonization and find ourselves once again.

The Importance of Being "In Between"

Growing up, I faced a lot of discrimination, from both the white kids and the other Latinx students. You see, I look Mexican, and my family is clearly Mexican given our *café con leche* skin and our dark hair and eyes. I would be profiled and called terrible words by the white kids, yet I was also looked down upon by the "real Mexicans," those who were actually from Mexico or whose parents had been immigrants. I didn't speak Spanish then, and even now I struggle with the language. Every time I come across a word in Spanish I don't know, English inevitably pops out of my mouth, filling the gaps. There's a metaphor there that I would desperately like to ignore but it's no use: *Spanglish*. Just like my blood, my speech encompasses the indigenous and colonizer alike.

My ancestors chose assimilation over preservation. My grandmother didn't learn Spanish and didn't pass it along to my mother who could have passed it to me. Somewhere between my great grandparents and my Grami, a choice was made for me and the rest of my family. I'm not sure what happened, but judging by the way my grandmother would do everything she could to be anything but Mexican—she wasn't fooling anybody—I can only assume it was traumatic. Much was lost in that event including pieces of our culture that might never return. It's because of this choice that I felt so very alone—as if I were the only person stuck between. Not white enough to fit in with the white kids and not Mexican enough to hang out with the Mexicans, it was incredibly isolating.

It wasn't until the last several years that I began to share this out loud: my story of life as someone who is in between, of what it's like to be both and neither. As I did so, my community surprised me once again by coming forward with their own stories of how their grandparents, parents, and other ancestors made the choice to assimilate for their own protection and the safety of their children. Yet in the process, they had to let go of our roots and culture. I realized I was not alone. My story was not new or unique. There is, in fact, an entire generation right now who is exactly where I am. We are Mexican and American all at once. We are filling the space between.

In witchcraft and magic there is a place—or more precisely an idea—called *liminal space*. A liminal space is a place that is in between two things or where two things meet. A crossroads is a liminal space because two roads intersect. If you stand in the center of the crossroads, which road are you on? Both and neither. Other liminal spaces are doorways (between inside and outside), the beach (between land and sea), twilight and dawn (between day and night), midnight (between two days), and there are many, many more. These liminal areas are widely considered to be extremely potent magical spaces. They act as doorways between our world and the next, where spirits may come through and interact with us to create powerful magic. We as Mexican Americans who are caught between our ancestral history as Mexicans and our personal future as Americans *are* a liminal space. Therefore, we are potent magical beings. Most of us are naturally psychic or otherwise "in tune," and it's not uncommon for us as liminal people to experience paranormal or supernatural phenomena more frequently than other folks.

We all carry the blood of our ancestors who lived in Mexico however many generations ago. You see, they knew things, powerful things. *Abuela* spent her life among creatures that most of the world would dismiss as legend, fairy tale, or myth. To her and her brothers and sisters, they were very real. And she and her family had very real ways of dealing with these supernatural neighbors of theirs. They learned to draw lines in the dirt between *los diablos* and *la familia* and how to communicate with the spirit world when they needed extra support. It's how they survived poverty, colonization, and every other hard stone life could throw at them.

Now that bloodline has left the Mexican countryside and ended up here in the United States, in you. Our grandparents' wisdom, stories, prayers, and faith are still alive in our magic. It's the foundation; it's our blood and our calling. But we aren't in Mexico anymore. We are in the United States, and this world is a whole new ball of wax. Our problems are very different and our personal flair for the work has come through in our new magic. We use words like *Latinx* and *Brujx*, get tattoos, and grow our nails long or wear our holy rosaries to complement our personal style. We are both Mexican and American now, and this book is here to guide you through the modern streets of the old magic.

Mexican people, even those outside this liminal generation, are inherently magical. I think it has something to do with the fact that Mexico is one of the few places where magic is still alive and well. In its culture, magic and superstition are still a part of our daily lives. We still have rituals to protect, heal, and bless ourselves and our families. Our culture maintains unique spirits, both *santo y oscuro*, as well as an unwavering faith in the Catholic saints, God, and Jesus Christ. This magic and these spirits did not leave us just because we immigrated and assimilated. Many of us in this generation of Mexican Americans are feeling a pull back to the magic of our ancestors. As liminal people we form the bridge between these two worlds, and as such it's up to us to heal the wounds of colonization, reclaim our heritage, and find that which was lost to us.

What Is American Brujeria?

American Brujeria (brew-hair-EE-yuh) is a term that I came up with to describe the folk magic that has been brought to the United States by Mexican immigrants. This work includes the lighting of novena candles, calling upon saints, the veneration of Our Lady of Guadalupe, spiritual cleansing through *limpias*, and the casting of spells known as *hechizos*. Since folks began crossing the border into the United States from Mexico, they have brought with them ancient wisdom, powerful spirits, techniques for healing and harming, and more. All of these bits and pieces of Mexico's deeply spiritual beliefs that were carried over on the backs of immigrants ended up being put into a large pile, mixing together into a singular practice that sustained our people over the years as folks now living in a foreign country. These were passed down through the generations and are ultimately how we ended up with American Brujeria.

This work is informed by traditional brujería (see below), Catholic belief, Aztec legend, Curanderismo (Mexican healing arts), and *Hechiceria* (sorcery). The practical and most utilitarian parts of these practices are what tend to survive in the United States as they are the parts that are most heavily leaned upon. What's more is that these have become so engrained in our culture as Mexican Americans that we often don't see these things as strange or in any way "magical"; it's just something you do. It's only after we really start to look around and examine our traditions that we realize how much magic we as Mexican and Mexican American folk are surrounded by every day. Italian and African cultures are much the same. In fact, over the years some techniques and themes from other forms of American folk magic, particularly Hoodoo, have influenced each other, and you'll often see a lot of crossover in our work.

Furthermore, American Brujeria has a habit of finding its way into the hands of Latinx folks living in the United States, and many people begin to do it without even realizing it. Especially among our young folks, there seems to be a big call happening, drawing Latinx youth back to their culture and traditional magical practices. It is also common among Latinx youth to refer to this work as *"brujería"* as a half joke with deadly serious undertones. Make no mistake, this work is powerful and should not be handled lightly.

How Are American Brujeria and Traditional Brujería Different?

Real traditional brujería is a very secretive tradition accessible to very few people. (When written correctly in Spanish, as opposed to Spanglish, Brujería has an acute accent over the *i*.) You must be mentored by a real brujo/a, and it is not a type of magic that you talk about openly. If you speak to your Mexican or Latinx friends, most of us have family stories about brujas. In researching this book I heard all kinds of astounding firsthand accounts of people flying or transforming into creatures like owls and jaguars. This magic is very real and very powerful and is most often used to harm or manipulate others. Furthermore, Brujería has very little to do with novena candles and saints—closer to a practice that we call *Hechiceria* (eh-chee-suh-REE-uh) or "sorcery." However the latter term is much less known, especially in the United States, and therefore seldom used. I also have a feeling that folks avoid using it because it is harder to say.

When you ask Mexican American folks what our mixed bag of folk magic is called, we will often refer to it as Brujería, again, sometimes as a joke, but it's what we continue to call it nonetheless. While this is traditionally inaccurate, there is a large tendency for folks to diverge from tradition after immigration—much like how you have Voodoo, Haitian Vodou, Puerto Rican Voodoo (Sanse), and New Orleans Voodoo. Still, it would be damaging to my culture to assert that this is real traditional Brujería. I wanted to help preserve the meaning of Brujería and I wanted to differentiate between the traditional kind and what we call Brujeria here in America. Thus, I coined the term *American Brujeria* to describe this unique path.

The Word Brujo/a/x

In the United States, there is a tendency for Latinx folks who practice the American Brujeria style of magic to refer to themselves as brujas (female witches), brujos (male witches), or *brujx*

(American gender-neutral term for witch). This creates a bit of a separation that can be hard to traverse when it comes to "Mexico style" or "American style" that really needs to be discussed and understood if we are going to call ourselves by these titles.

The first thing we have to understand is that the words mean different things depending on where you are geographically. In Mexico there is a lot of fear surrounding brujas and brujos, and if you say you are one of those, folks will immediately try to distance themselves from you—if not literally run away. You have to be careful how you use this word because in the United States our modern use of the word *witch* has become very dewy-eyed and we often understand witches as "spiritual healers who love the earth." Meanwhile in Mexico, if you tell someone you are a bruja/o, you are telling them that you like to fly through the night and steal babies and eat them. Our understanding of these terms differs in the extreme. In the United States, for example, if someone calls themselves a bruja/o/x, they are simply saying that they are a Latinx person who practices a Latinx style of magic. It's also considered incorrect in traditional Mexican culture to refer to yourself as bruja/o if you are not practicing *real* Mexican Brujería. Those who practice American Brujeria are much closer to what we'd call an *hechicero/a/x*; however most folks favor brujo/a/x as a personal title. This brings us to an important point: since using brujo/a/x is intentionally incorrect, we must realize that makes it politically charged. Those from outside of the community should think twice before applying the title to themselves. It's a little like how Native Americans may call themselves and each other "Indians," yet it's not considered acceptable for folks from outside of the community to talk in the same manner.

Language is complicated and the meanings of words change across geographical landscape, periods of time, and regional dialects. Due to this, I don't think it's inherently wrong to use brujo/a/x to describe a person who works in American Brujeria as long as you understand the nuances and roots and realize that there is a time and place where it is best to not identify this way.

Wielding History

When I began collecting stories from my community, I could see the common threads that tied us all together and the fascinating and sometimes comical differences from person to person. This is a living, breathing tradition that's growing, changing, and expanding every moment. Even from house to house and family to family, there are nuances and differences. *Limpia con huevo* (cleansing with an egg) is done on Tuesdays and Thursdays in some families, but on Sundays in others. Some don't care what day it is, but the egg *must* be room temperature. Still others say the egg must be cold. You see, it's fluid and changes with you and your family's history.

I'll teach you how to do the *limpia con huevo* the way I do it, but listen to your *tías* and your *abuelas* on the subtleties. If they say, *"sólo los martes y jueves,"* then follow that. That has power! When you follow a practice the way your family has done it traditionally over the generations, then you aren't just wielding an egg, you are wielding history. Your ancestors are suddenly holding the egg with you, and the prayers of your grandmothers surround you as you carry on that tradition. If your family has lost the knowledge or there is no one left to teach you, find your preferred methods and pass them on. Don't forget that tradition and history can start with us.

Can Non-Mexicans Use This Magic?

Yes, absolutely! Just about anyone can use the techniques taught in this book for their own magical purposes. I believe we should be learning about and from other cultures in order to have an expanded worldview. I'm also not against folks taking bits and pieces of this world and bringing it back to their own personal craft, even if they aren't strictly practicing American Brujeria. *However*, I know that a lot of folks coming from outside the community want to practice this magic respectfully. I can appreciate that, and I want to help guide you through handling someone else's culture with respect and grace.

The first thing you need to understand is that you are a guest in this world, and your job as a guest is to be on your best behavior. Cultural appropriation is a big issue these days, especially within the world of spirituality where, as history tells us, some folks think that other people's cultures are up for grabs. Please remember that when you are approaching ethnic forms of spirituality, it is best to remain a follower of tradition. This is how we preserve precious culture.

Our magic and our spirits—*Santa Muerte* included—belong to us as the descendants of Mexico, as do our spiritual titles. Learning the techniques in this book does not make you a *brujx* or *curandero*. These titles really mean something to us and shouldn't be adopted haphazardly, especially by those from outside of the community. Only if you truly learn the traditions and uphold them the way they were meant to be, *and* the local Mexican community begins to refer to you as such, may you then adopt that title proudly. Most folks don't know about that last part. In Mexican culture, even those with complete educations in something like Curanderismo don't refer to themselves as *curanderos* until the community bestows the title upon them.

Furthermore, you cannot actively participate in racism against a community whose magic you are using. Our powerful spirits are watching and listening and will respond accordingly. It is safest to refrain from this work until you are ready and willing to protect and support the community you are borrowing magic from. If you are voting, speaking, or engaging in any activity that actively harms, belittles, or otherwise endangers Mexican communities, you have no business participating in our traditions. So before you begin this work, I recommend a little introspection. Are you a good ally to the Mexican community? If not, what changes do you intend to make to fix that? These are important questions we should all be asking ourselves and then following through with meaningful action. Please remember that being a good ally is work that doesn't end; you must actively do it every day.

If you approach this work with respect and reverence, we are happy to have you among us. Mexicans as a whole tend to be a welcoming people full of warmth and joy, and as long as you aren't causing any problems, we are glad to share with you. I know many non-Mexican Americans who love this work but often come to me absolutely terrified that they might be appropriating my culture. If this describes you, there are three simple guidelines for avoiding cultural insensitivity while engaging in this work:

- First, this work should not make you money or at least not in any meaningful way. Profiting from cultures that are not your own is wrong. This doesn't mean that you can't charge for your services, it just means to be careful about exploiting the knowledge for profit. Remember this is a style of magic made by and for poor and marginalized communities. What you charge and what you make should reflect that, and these services should remain accessible to the Latinx population. For instance, it's become very common to see non-Latinx charging hundreds of dollars for a "*limpia.*" This means they are profiting off our ancestral magic while simultaneously making it inaccessible to our people.

- Second, you shouldn't take up space in Mexican communities. For instance, if you are a non-Mexican, you should avoid showing up at a Mexican market selling your *Santa Muerte* statues. You are most likely taking up a spot that could otherwise belong to an *abuela* trying to sell enough tamales to keep her lights on. You also shouldn't teach this magic or educate others on it publicly—leave that to Mexican folk. You may, however, attend the market and the classes to show support.

- Third, your actions shouldn't erase culture. This happens frequently, and folks don't even realize they are doing it. Say you are Wiccan—no shade, Wicca is awesome—and you notice that Mexican folk pray to *La Virgen de Guadalupe* and you want to as well. That's great! Absolutely fine. However, if you begin doing traditional Wicca with a statue of Guadalupe thrown in and start calling it *brujería*, then we have a problem. Not only is that incorrect, but these things have a habit of spreading. Then suddenly everyone is doing fake *brujería* thinking what they have is the real deal, and it begins erasing the actual tradition as more and more folks come to believe they are doing it correctly. The same goes for when people from outside of the community try to get creative with the work and therefore begin changing it. For example, this happens when folks realize that Hoodoo uses jars in some spells. The next thing you know there's a book out by a non-African American author on "Hoodoo jar spells" detailing rituals with jars full of glitter that are not actually Hoodoo at all. Lastly, bending the rules to make something easier is also a popular way folks like to erase culture. For instance, folks want to be involved in Santería, but it's a lot of work. So they decide to skip all the hard stuff and go straight to lighting candles to Oshun without observing centuries of tradition. The erasure of culture usually happens inadvertently, when folks get too excited while studying someone else's magic.

If you are following these three simple rules, you should be just fine. Welcome to our world!

The Basics

Throughout my time working with American Brujeria, I've come to understand that our power comes from three main places. The first is our faith. Our belief and connection with higher spirits such as God, Jesus Christ, *La Virgen y Los Santos* are a huge source of power, protection, and wisdom. Our grandmothers would arm themselves like soldiers with the cross, holy water, prayers, and saints' medals. The only person *El Diablo* is afraid of on earth is an *abuela*. She is so fearsome because she knows she has backup. She has *Dios y Los Santos* by her side, and she is not about to be messed with. Faith is a powerful thing that we must never take for granted as it is the cornerstone of all magic.

The second place our power comes from is the earth—*la tierra*. Mexican people have a powerful connection with their Great Mother. She provides us with plants, stones, and the mud from which we built our houses. We nourish ourselves with food grown from her body, and we give our bodies back to her when we die. She holds the ancestors that rest below our feet. We see her in recipes from our grandmothers: certain types of corn for these tamales, these plants for a poultice for that rash, these roots and tree barks to scare away evil, and so on and so forth. The land is omnipresent in our work, just like God or *La Virgen* (who is sacred to the earth, but we'll discuss that later). It's easy to forget about the earth; we as a people spend a lot of time looking up. But we know she's still there, cradling our knees while we pray to the heavens.

The third and final source that our magic draws power from is our families. Growing up Mexican, you quickly learn the power of *la familia*. True, sometimes they can be a major pain, yet when we need them the most, they are here for us. Our families are often our first line of defense when we need advice or comfort. When we are facing problems, where do we go? We go to *la familia*. A lot of this folk magic is passed down through the family line, which is how we get so many different ways of doing things. I'm certain some of you will read this book and think, "Well, that's not how my *abuela* did it," and that's fine because everyone's *abuela* did it differently and you may even catch them arguing with each other on the best ways to do things. This is part of the living, breathing tradition. But the methods *our particular* family used hold special power. These techniques have been tested by generations of your ancestors. These ancestors remain in these traditions and empower them even further. Imagine if you will your grandmother's special apple pie. You may find recipes that make a better-tasting pie, but it's not the same. Her recipe is special because it's hers, and it carries a special magic that no other pie seems to have. This is a concept I'll repeat many times through this book. Your hand making the sign of the cross with the egg like your *abuela* taught you isn't just your hand anymore: it's her hand too, and her mother's hand that taught her, and her mother's father's hand, and his father's before him. Yes, it's not just the *abuelas*; the *abuelos* and *tíos* are there too. This power emanating from the family is extremely potent, and it amplifies the other two powers of faith and earth by providing tradition.

With these three pillars, it's easy to see how and why this magic works so well. They provide a connection with the divine, materials to work with, and tried-and-true rituals that guide our hands while we weave this powerful magic. In this chapter we will cover the concepts that are unique to this practice, as well as the tools used and how they operate. In later chapters we will revisit most of them as we talk about their practical applications. Let's begin . . .

The Concepts

Bitter and Sweet

In this work, most things will be split up into two categories: things that are bitter and things that are sweet. Bitter things have a harsh and cutting energy. These include things like bitter-tasting plants and herbs, sour fruits, harsh-smelling incenses, sharp or pointy objects; even startling sounds can be considered bitter. This energy is most often employed to chase something away.

Bitter isn't always bad, though. Usually things that are considered bitter are the most cleansing and protective energies. They really cut through negativity like a knife. When faced with some pretty heavy energy, a *curandero* might prescribe you a "bitter bath" to cleanse you. This is often a cold bath—cold is considered bitter—made with herbs like rue, lemons, limes, holy basil, coffee, and/or salt to strip away the evil. I personally like to use white vinegar in these baths as well for the same reason, but we'll talk more about *baños* later.

Sweet things are often used as a lure for spirits and good energies. These are things that can be sweet-tasting, good-smelling, or pleasing to look at. This encompasses flowers, honey, milk, cologne, soft things, warm things, and comforting things. Burning incense that smells sweet attracts good spirits. Sweet things can be used for cleansing, but they are not as powerful as bitter things. For instance, say you were beginning to smell really bad and needed a bath. You could use perfume (sweet) to cover the smell, and this might work nicely the first day or two. But then, after a while, it's not enough and you're simply just trying to mask a larger problem. Eventually you'll need to use soap (bitter) to cut through all the filth. Sweet things are often really nice to use after bitter things to soothe, comfort, and bring in good energies to the spirit after it's been scrubbed raw by something like a bitter bath. The two often work well in tandem.

The Bible and More

Although modern individual beliefs vary, traditional Mexican culture is Catholic-based. It's part of that whole colonization thing that we had to go through. When the Spanish introduced the Bible and Catholicism to the indigenous people of Mexico, they had already formed a wide and complex view of the divine. In comparison, something like the Bible seems very small and overly simple. After all, it is just one book, and though it is complex and fascinating, no single book is large enough to contain all of God's mysteries. When we as a people were forcibly converted to Christianity, we eventually grabbed hold of the Bible and its stories like a life raft and made them our own. However, you can't erase thousands of years of experience with the other realms. The Aztecs, Maya, and other civilizations throughout Latin America were extremely spiritual, and we had already made contact with so many spirits and deities. We came to believe the stories in the

Bible, of course, and we learned to accept Jesus Christ as our Lord and Savior. We got right with *El Espíritu Santo*. However, we knew that those stories and that book encompassed only a small slice of the vast unending mysteries of our world. After all, the Bible says nothing about the cactus plant, and yet we know they exist. Furthermore, Mexico has seen some desperate times, and in these moments folks were pushed to search outside of mainstream Catholicism for help. Even the most devout have been forced to seek aid from forces the Church may not approve of. We as a people will do what needs to be done to survive, and this includes supplementing our faith in God with the knowledge of folk traditions.

We often call this type of belief folk Catholicism, which is essentially the integration of pre-Christian rituals and beliefs with Catholicism. I like to call it "Catholic plus," which is Catholicism plus the long-held Pagan stories, beliefs, and superstitions. This confuses a lot of people, but after a while you get the hang of it. The key is to realize that God can't ever be squeezed into a neat little package. So, while conventional American Catholics may reject the idea of things like ghosts, witches, *La Llorona*, etc., those of us with Mexican roots know that they are in fact very real. Many of us have seen them or had experiences with them. This innate cultural superstition is part of what makes us so magical.

Now, I'm sure you're wondering if you have to be a Catholic to do this work, and the answer is no. You do not have to be or consider yourself Catholic. You don't have to go to church on Sunday or get baptized—no, none of that. However, you do have to *believe*. If you are going to pray to St. Michael, you must have faith he is real and can help you. When you pray the rosary to the Virgin Mary, you must know that she is there watching over you, or else your prayers will fall like dust. Some folks like to take American folk magic techniques and apply Pagan gods to them.

This can be tricky, and you risk offending certain spirits. If you want to take the techniques from this book and sub in Hekate for *La Virgen*, I can't stop you, but realize once you do that you are no longer practicing American Brujeria, and you should not refer to it as such. You are practicing something adjacent to it, but it's no longer Mexican American folk magic.

Prayer

I love prayer. Prayer can be a very intense experience, and the act of reaching up toward God is something that I feel is too easily discounted. In American Brujeria we weave our spells in prayer because that's how our ancestors were taught to do it. When we pray, we are connecting straight to God, *La Virgen,* or the ancestors. This is extremely powerful, but folks just write it off because it's so simple. Let me tell you, though: if you can learn to do it right, prayer is stronger than any rhyming incantation you can use. Incantations can be fun and helpful for speaking your intention into the universe, but if you can dial direct, all the better!

Learning to pray is simple. Don't be afraid. Remember that God and *La Virgen* already know all about you, so you can relax. All the cats are out of the bag and the skeletons are out of every closet. They've watched you grow up and are basically the most invested *tío* and *tía* you've ever had. They are family—so speak to them that way. Try to be respectful, but don't get too worried about presentation when you're just starting out. God has a sense of humor, for sure. I mean look at the platypus—need I say more? Anyway, begin however you would like, then just pour your heart out. Speak freely and openly with them. When you are done, make sure to close the prayer with something. *Amen* is fine and popular, or you can let them know that you're "signing off"—it doesn't matter much. I do think it's important to have a greeting and a closing though because, let's face it, God and *La*

Virgen have a lot going on. I find that having an open and close lets them know when they need to be paying attention and when you're finished so they can resume tending to the multiverse.

We must remember that we are active participants in prayer. We must put energy into it because we are trying to make something happen. This doesn't mean we must use force, and muscle our way to the divine. I find even the most delicate prayers can be extremely powerful. The point is to open a connection between yourself and God. We can't do that if we are being dishonest, pushy, or insincere. We have to mean it when we pray. Now, I know that if you are new to prayer, it can seem a little funny—like you're talking to an imaginary friend. If you feel weird or disconnected, simply ask God or *La Virgen* to come closer to you while you pray. Don't forget to reach upward with your words and energy when you pray, because when we reach up, the divine reaches down to us as well. I do this first by being extremely sincere. The purer our words are, the faster we form the connection. You can also help facilitate this by visualizing the spirit or vibration of your words floating up and creating that connection and opening that channel like a bridge.

Speak from the heart when you pray. I rarely have something preplanned, and you don't have to pray any certain way either. Just begin speaking to God or *La Virgen*. What do you want them to know? Maybe it's just stopping in to say thanks for the beautiful weather that day. Maybe it's just to tell them how nervous you are for an exam you have coming up. It doesn't matter: just be sincere, and really feel what it is that you are saying. If you stutter or don't feel like you are being eloquent, don't worry, the divine understands us perfectly because they don't listen to our words. They listen to our hearts and how we are feeling in them. If you are saying a prayer of gratitude, really dive into the emotion of gratitude. If you are saying a prayer for a future event you are nervous about, try to relax as you speak to them. Feel your burdens shift into their hands and then have faith.

Prayer doesn't always have to be to God or *La Virgen*. It can be to *Los Santos*, or even to our own ancestors who have passed on. Prayer creates a bridge between all worlds and is used the same exact way in every instance. So feel free to reach out to your helpers, guides, and protectors on the other side this way. Create that link so that they can be part of this life with you. The more you pray—whether it's to God or your Great Grandma Juanita— the stronger the connection becomes and the more you'll feel their presence linger even after you've finished.

In American Brujeria, it's very common to use certain pre-written prayers for just about everything. For instance, the *Padre Nuestro* (Our Father) and the *Dios te Salve, María* (Hail Mary) can be applied to nearly any purpose you can think of. So if you aren't great at freestyling, especially when under pressure, you can always fall back on these traditional prayers. You may do them in English if that is most comfortable for you, but learning them in Spanish brings in the power of tradition and helps you tap into the power of your ancestors. We'll review both later on.

Blessing

Most things in this work need to be blessed in one way or another. This is what gives them power and makes them holy. Essentially, blessing is the act of bringing something in contact with the divine, and this fleeting contact leaves behind a light and a power in the object for us to work with. Blessing is simple and can be done in any number of ways. You may pray over the object with words from the heart or pre-written prayers like the *Padre Nuestro* or the *Dios te Salve*. You may also sprinkle objects with holy water. Holy water is blessed and its blessings can transfer to other things. I am also a fan of making the sign of the cross over an object and calling upon the Holy Trinity (Father, Son, and Holy Spirit) as a means of blessing. You may make the sign of the cross one time or three times depending on your personal preference. It's also important that whatever you are blessing be cleansed first. Some things like holy water pull double duty and both purify and bless whatever they come in contact with. Still, I like to start with a cleansed object either way. Natural objects such as herbs and stones don't necessarily need blessing, but I still like to do it to boost their natural powers, and I pray over them to speak to their spirits.

Cleansing

Most new tools or items used in your work will need a cleansing. The idea is that before that item got to you, it came in contact with a lot of people and energies and might be contaminated. By cleansing it, we essentially empty it of everything it has picked up, and then we can fill it with our own energies and intentions. It's simple to do, and there are many ways to go about it—so you're bound to find a way that works for you. Some common methods use salt or salt water: you may sprinkle salt on an object or soak it in salt water to cleanse it. You may also run the object through the smoke from cleansing herbs or resins such as copal, sage, rue, or other plants. You may run it under cold water or let it sit in the sun. You may wash it with holy water or Florida Water. These are just a few of the ways to cleanse an object, but they are the most easily accessible for everyday folks. Cleansing homes and spaces was something our ancestors did to prevent sickness, misfortune, and death—more on that later.

Mal de Ojo

Like most cultures, we believe in *Mal de Ojo*, or *Ojo* for short. This is what others call the evil eye, or a blast of negativity sent to you by someone's jealous glance. Such harm can come from friends, family, strangers, or enemies who look upon you with envy or malice. *Ojo* is easily contracted and arguably the most common form of psychic/magical attack a person will face in their lifetime. The symptoms include headache, nausea, fatigue, fainting, seizures, sudden illness, bad luck, crossed (jinxed) conditions, and more. What most people don't know is that it's easiest for friends and family to give *Ojo* to one another, and it's often transmitted by a compliment. Someone who comes up to you and says, "I love your hair, it's so beautiful! I wish I had hair like that . . ." is likely inadvertently giving you *Ojo*, especially if their own hair is thinning or unbeautiful in some way.

There are many ways to cure an attack of *Mal de Ojo*. In Mexican culture it is often believed that if the person touches you while they say it, it neutralizes the effect by sort of grounding it like electricity. I don't find this to be true and have often felt that the touch intensifies the effect of *Ojo* instead. When you have been given *Ojo* by someone, it's often important to work quickly. A *limpia con huevo* is a very common method of removing it, as are *barridas* or *baños* with plants like rue, which has a particular affinity for removing and blocking *Mal de Ojo*. See the chapter on *Limpias* for more information.

The Tools

Copal

Copal is extremely important in Mexican spirituality. It is a resin that comes from trees in the torchwood family, closely related to frankincense and myrrh. The Aztecs used to burn huge amounts of it as a gift for their gods. Mostly in today's world we turn to it for its powers of blessing, cleansing, and empowering. The smoke can bless and empower magical objects we intend to use in our practice. It can be employed to chase out evil entities and purify a space or object of unwanted energies. The smoke can be a divinatory tool. Observing shapes within its dips and twists may provide the insight you have been seeking. Its smoke can be used in healing to remove blockages and cure stagnation in a person's energy. It is also an excellent offering to any and all Mexican deities and spirits. Most of the time I use white copal because I find it to be all-purpose, but there are three main varieties.

The most common type I find is the white copal. It is very similar to frankincense in both energy and fragrance, and I often use them interchangeably due to this. I find both uplifting, purifying, and able to call in good spirits. My ancestors and spirits seem to enjoy it as an offering, and I burn it for them on special occasions. (Remember, sacred herbs and resins are not for daily use, but only for special occasions.) White copal is what I use for cleansing and purifying the most. It's also the type I would apply for healing work, as well as blessing.

The other two types are black copal, which carries a richer, darker, heavier scent, and golden copal, which is the sweetest and most decadent of the three. White copal smells the brightest—if that makes sense. Black copal, due to its heavier nature, is good for grounding spaces. It's also better for weightier or darker work. No copal is evil or negative in nature, but if you are about to bring a hammer down with your magic, black copal may be the way to go. Golden copal, due to its rich sweet scent and energy, is a great choice to burn as an offering to your deities. It's sure to please!

Sage and Smoke

There's a lot of controversy around sage right now and who should and should not be using it. I'm not here to get into that.

I'm only here to tell you what I know. Use your personal moral compass to decide what is best for you and your path given your place in society. What I can tell you, though, is Mexico is no stranger to the use of all kinds of bundled herbs for smoke cleansing, sage included. Most of us know that the burning of sage bundles is specifically a Native American practice, but we have to remember that Mexican people are the product of Native American and Spanish peoples coming together. Many Mexican folks, especially from the northern portion of the country, are indigenous Native American people who traditionally used plants like sage in their rituals. My grandmother was the first person to teach me how to do this. She used to sage down every new person that walked through her door as a blessing to them. She used blue desert sage, which is still my favorite. I find it less harsh than white sage, and it has a nice calm, sweet smell that is both cleansing and a draw for good energies. You should also make a habit of exploring the many alternative cleansing herbs sold in similar bundle (rosemary, juniper, etc.); they each have unique and powerful properties that you may like better than white sage. If you are going to use sage of any variety, do your best to make sure it is ethically sourced, or grow it yourself if you can. Remember to use it sparingly; sacred plants and resins should be used only when necessary. These are not to be turned to daily or on a whim. This powerful magic needs to be respected and preserved.

Like most practices in Mexican American folk magic, the art has been Christianized. It's common to find people who pray over their smoke bundles or take them to mass for blessing. A lot of folks pray while they burn it and make the sign of the cross with the smoke for extra potency. Lean into this practice of embracing holy power, and it will not steer you wrong.

Ruda

Ruda, or rue in English, is a powerful plant and highly revered in American Brujeria as a fierce protector. I consider her to be in a class I have come to call "Crone plants," which includes other herbs such as mugwort and nettle. These plants carry a deep wisdom and are quite serious in nature. Rue can be added to baths, burned, hung in the home, used as a sweep for *limpias*, and even be found in special soap bars that are great to take with you when traveling for an easy cleansing on the road. Many people plant rue by their front door to protect the home and bring in good energy. Rue not only safeguards against malefic witchcraft; it is also adept at removing spells that have already been cast on you. It is known to have a very special affinity for removing and repelling *Mal de Ojo* as well. Carrying rue, or even images of rue, will protect you and your family from all kinds of spiritual attacks. Remember that *ruda* is a powerful bitter and should be handled carefully. Those who are pregnant, trying to become pregnant, or breastfeeding should not have contact with this plant.

Florida Water

Florida Water is not actually water at all, it's a cologne. It is used all throughout Latinx, African American, and Caribbean traditions as a deep cleanser of negative energies, a lifter of vibration, and an offering for spirits. I keep some in a spray bottle mixed with holy water and spray myself down before spiritual work and use it to clean off my tools and altar space when necessary. Its floral fragrance attracts good spirits and energies and also chases off the bad ones. Since it's alcohol-based, it is flammable, so be careful with it around candles. We also exploit its flammability for certain types of fire *limpias* we will discuss later.

Red Ribbon

Red ribbon, yarn, string, or cord is employed all over the world—and mostly for the same reason. Red is a powerful color that represents strength, protection, and luck, among other things. Red ribbon is commonly used in American Brujeria for its powers of protection. Tied around the wrists or the hands, it keeps the worker from picking up negative energy from clients or objects. Red ribbon can also be placed around the home to protect against unhealthy or evil energies; thus when hung in or around a doorway it will repel any evil that tries to enter your home. Worn at the wrist or around the neck, it protects against *Mal de Ojo*.

Candles

Las velas are crucial in American Brujeria. We've all seen them at one point or another: tall glass tubes with flames flickering away inside of them, doing the work of the faithful. These candles are extremely powerful and well-loved throughout Mexican and Mexican American culture. We'll get into the details on which kinds may be available, as well as how to use them, in a later chapter, but I wanted to touch on them here.

Vigil candles, or novenas, come from an old Roman funeral practice that was later adopted by the Catholic Church and brought to Mexico. Since then they have become ingrained in our culture. Traditionally they were mostly dedicated to saints, which we still see today. However, in the 1970s and '80s we began to see intention novenas, or novena candles that were not dedicated to a saint but to a purpose. For instance, there are Come to Me candles, which help draw in a lover, or Court Case candles, which assist with legal matters. These, though fairly modern, are extremely effective and have quickly become a favorite tool in American Brujeria. More to come on that later.

Though we associate Mexican magic with novenas, regular stick candles are not to be dismissed. Even just a plain white candle can pack a serious wallop in the hands of an experienced worker! Never underestimate the simple parts of this work—for they are where the real power lies. Some workers use only white candles; others prefer to work with certain colors for certain purposes. It truly does not matter, and you will find your own preference or maybe cycle through using just white candles or color candles over your lifetime. It all works.

Condition Oils

American Brujeria borrows from other American forms of folk magic. That's part of folk magic: you share with your neighbors, and over time, it all begins to overlap. Condition oils are no exception and are found basically everywhere there is magic backed by Abrahamic religions. These oils are infused with herbs, roots, stones, and the energy of religious objects and other curios to instill a certain power in them. These oils can then be used in a nearly infinite number of ways. You may anoint yourself to bring protection, love, or blessings. You may anoint candles to enhance their power. You may anoint doorways and windows to protect from evil. Truly the sky is the limit, and there is an oil for just about everything!

Holy Water

Holy water is an extremely useful substance, and it's easy to come by! Most churches will give it to you for free, or you may bring bottles—or even gallons—of water to a priest and ask for them to be blessed. Holy water is particularly adept at chasing away devils and demons, as well as imparting holy power to everything it touches. This means that if we need to bless something with holy power, we may bring it in contact with holy water and say a prayer. Simple as that, the blessing is complete. Small bottles of holy water may be placed around the home to offer protection. Some folks place the bottles in windowsills, above doorframes, or under beds. Others add holy water to their window cleaner and wash their windows with it to protect the home.

Scissors, Horseshoes, and Garlic

Household items such as scissors are used frequently in this work to defend against evil. Not only do scissors make an X when opened—a symbol of blocking—they also sport fierce points to pierce *Ojo* and cut up anything else that might be sent your way. Other items such as horseshoes and garlic are also used to ward off evil and sickness.

2

La Iglesia

The Church is a place of power. It's where we go to connect with God, Jesus, *La Virgen*, and *El Espíritu Santo*. It's full of prayers, and spiritual power is just hanging in the air. It vibrates in the still silence with the echoes of muffled footsteps and muttered devotions. It is here, in this holy place, where we may speak to God and light a candle. As a child I would watch the people from my church, the ones who looked like me, do these simple rituals. I remember the old *abuelitas* with their shawls wrapped around them, lighting votive candles in their little red holders and whispering prayers. Or were they *spells*?

To be honest, I've never really been sure there's a difference. Even with their gnarled hands and their backs hunched with age, these women seemed powerful. More than that, they all seemed to know something the rest of us didn't. I grew up in a mostly white area, and those folks didn't seem to *get it* on the level the *abuelas* did. It was as if God were right next to them, like they could conjure Jesus right there in the church. I wanted to know their secrets and how they came to be so faithful.

Near where I live now is a Catholic abbey. It sits up in the hills and houses a Benedictine order of monks. The church itself and the grounds are stunning. There are small shrines and altars hidden all over the place. That's where you may find the spiritual work of the local Mexican American population—myself included. Novena candles, flowers, coins and other types of offerings, prayers, and works are left here for either a saint or *La Virgen*. I learned a lot from the everyday Mexican women who visit this place. Their prayers are so strong. The abbey has a long winding road leading up to it, and the stone shrine to *La Virgen* is hidden off to the side. I once watched a woman pull her car over and get out with a huge grocery bag full of novena candles. She started praying from the moment she got out of the car, crossing herself and muttering before she even began to walk. She carried her prayers all the way to the shrine where she crossed herself with each candle before setting them on the altar. This woman and others like her taught me to connect with God by praying like I mean it. I got to see how they placed their novenas, paid for their favors, and settled their debts. They all understood that *la iglesia* is a holy place and doing work in a holy place is powerful. It sets the work in God's house and delivers us directly into His hands.

Working in the Church

Now, some churches you can work in, and others you cannot. You may have to look around for a work-friendly church, but if you are in a place with a high Latinx population, it shouldn't be too difficult. Many Catholic churches have candle stations where you can burn your novenas. Sometimes they are in a little rack that sits outside by the doors of the church or a little bit inside. Sometimes—unfortunately—they are at the very front near the altar. You may have to look around a bit, but there's usually a place for novenas. You may also charge and bless items in the church before using them in your work somewhere else.

Candles in the Church

If your church does have a novena rack, then you may feel free to bring those in and burn them in the church. Sometimes the rack stays outside, or there might be an outdoor shrine—usually to some form of Mary—where you may burn them as well. These are preferred because they are a little safer and usually made of stone. Plus nature and open air have their own merits for certain *hechizos*. I'm not sure about where you are, but around here it's a custom to place the candles with their front label facing the statue or the icon of the saint the shrine is dedicated to. This way you are showing them precisely what it is you want—not to mention the prayers you need access to are on the back of the candles where you can see them. I'm lucky that in the church where I do my work, we have both an outdoor shrine to *La Virgen* and many paintings of saints lining the interior walls. Each of these paintings has a wide marble table jutting out just below it for novena candles.

Some folks simply pray over their novenas and others like to dress them with herbs and oils. If you are in the latter group, make sure to dress them at home beforehand; don't do that in the church. We'll talk more about these candles in a later chapter. If you are doing this type of candle work in the church, be sure to use only saints' candles or plain unlabeled candles because church workers maintaining the shrines and disposing of the spent candles and offerings will notice if you bring in something that looks witchy.

If no racks for novenas are provided, your second-best option is the rack for votive candles. These are extremely common in

Catholic churches and easy to work with discreetly. Just striking a match and saying a meaningful prayer are generally enough to get the job done when you are in the house of God. However, with proper discretion, slightly more complex works can be done. If you would like to bless your candle or touch it to yourself, that's generally okay. Just keep it low-key. The church is a peaceful place, and if you make a scene—or go noticed at all—you're going to look like a fool and most likely won't be welcomed back.

We must remember that the most important parts of this work are simply prayer, faith, and lighting the candle. But most folks want something a little more exciting. Here are some ideas for working discreetly with the votive rack.

When you walk into the church, there's usually a pedestal containing holy water for you to bless yourself with before going all the way in. This is an excellent opportunity to bless something you've brought with you too. Maybe it's a saint's medal, or maybe it's a candle you've carried from home. Either way, it doesn't look too strange to cross yourself with it, then touch something in your palm. Bringing a candle from home can be helpful as it gives you more time to anoint or bless the candle in privacy beforehand. I recommend finding out what type of candles they use at that church first though. Some use only tea lights because they are easier to change out, so if you melt a full votive in the glass holder, it will be noticed. I also do not recommend using dried herbs for these candles because they tend to catch fire and produce a large flame. You don't want to be halfway through mass only to see a little bonfire action in the corner of the room. It's not safe, something could catch fire—or worse, you could get the giggles in church. Either way, don't risk it.

You may choose to go straight from the holy water to the votive rack and use a candle already there. When working at the votive rack, you can also pick up the candle and make the sign of the cross over it to bless it and empower it or cross yourself with the candle. For instance, if I'm going to be asking for protection, I'll bring a little holy water on my fingers and make the sign of the cross on the candle while praying and visualizing the candle glowing bright white. Then I'll cross myself with the candle to symbolize protection, deliverance, blessing, or healing upon myself and then light it. This can generally be done pretty unobtrusively. You can also purify the candle with a simple prayer as well. If you are shy, you can often work in churches during the day when not many people are around and/or a mass is not happening. That is the best time because you have more privacy, but still remember to be discreet.

Charging Items in the Church

It's also common for folks to bring items to mass that they intend to use for their work later. Back in the old days *curanderas* used to bring the plants for their *limpias y remedios* to mass with them. Some say even the famous Mexican healer Maria Sabina herself brought her sacred mushrooms to the church before using them in her visionary ceremonies. You may choose to bring candles with you, small bags or bundles of herbs, or other small things that won't be noticed. Generally the idea is the energy generated by so many people in prayer at once, along with your own direct prayers and intentions, will imbue the items with holy power.

It doesn't have quite the same effect if you just carry them into an empty church, but if you wanted to make yours a solo trip, you can still get a positive effect. I would begin by stopping at the holy water when you first walk in. Bless yourself, and sprinkle the water on whatever objects you brought. Make your way into the church, and light a votive if you can. This helps to capture God's attention and acts as an offering, but it's not essential if you are uncomfortable going up to the rack. Find an empty pew where you won't be disturbed. I get on my knees to pray, holding the small bundle of items between my palms. Praying sincerely and with power is important when doing this work. I generally say three Our Fathers, ask for blessings upon my items, and then close with three Hail Marys.

If you are going to mass, simply having the items on you when you are there is enough, but some folks like to ask for a blessing from the priest. If the items are small, I like to hold them in my dominant hand for most of mass but will pocket them if they become cumbersome or I need to use my hand to make contact with others during the service.

Remember when doing your work in the church to be discreet. You are in a house of God, and your main job is to go unnoticed. Most of us coming from a Latinx background were raised Catholic. If you were not and you wish to work in a Catholic church, I highly recommend doing some research and getting baptized if possible. All places have spirits, including churches, and they may mistake you for a foe if you come in asking for things without a membership card. Also, let's be honest, the church isn't going to give you anything if you don't have any faith or understanding: a connection to God and Jesus has to be there. If you are not on that wavelength and are stepping into a church for the first time ever to ask God for money or a boyfriend, you are going to be in trouble. Spirit doesn't just come running to fix us because we beckon. We need to be sincere, and we need to put in the work. So if you were raised outside of the Christian faith or have not healed your relationship with your Christian or Catholic upbringing, you need to forge that connection first before you get anywhere close to working in the church. It's like going into someone's house you don't know and expecting them to give you stuff. As colonized people, we know that is just plain rude.

Apart from working inside the church, you may also get magical tools from the church that are quite powerful. For instance, saints' medals, especially blessed ones, are incredibly potent for protection and spiritual strength. You may get rosaries and candles from the church as well. Holy water is generally distributed freely in such spaces, and some even have faucets or dispensers so that you can bring your own bottle to get some for use outside the church. On Epiphany they often give out blessed chalk, and sometimes on Candlemas they give out blessed candles. Palm Sunday is an excellent day to craft crosses out of the blessed palms to use as powerful protective charms. All of these things are valuable tools to add to your collection. If you form a relationship with the priest, he is usually happy to bless medals and other religious objects. But again, don't be weird.

Prayers

Prayer is a very important and powerful tool in the arsenal of American Brujeria. It's how we connect with the divine and draw down the power of God, Jesus, and *La Virgen*. Most of the time I encourage praying words from the heart, but in certain instances when we may be full of fear or sorrow, it's nice to have some traditional prayers to lean on. In my experience, it doesn't necessarily matter which traditional prayer you decide to use as most of them are generally considered multipurpose. The ones I will be sharing here in both English and Spanish are the standards and can be used for any occasion. I'm also adding a prayer to St. Michael that comes in handy specifically for protection in all situations. If you don't already speak Spanish, learning these in English first is good, but remember to challenge yourself with the Spanish too. Much like doing things the way your ancestors did them, praying in their tongue adds another level of power to your work.

El Padre Nuestro

The first traditional prayer we will cover here is commonly known in English as the Our Father, or in Spanish *El Padre Nuestro*. Recite this anytime you need God for anything. You need a blessing? *Padre Nuestro*. You need protection? *Padre Nuestro*. You gotta kick *El Diablo* out of *la casa*? *Padre Nuestro*. I personally use this prayer as I do healing work, and I open and close all my prayer sessions with it.

Our Father

Our Father, who art in heaven,
hallowed be thy Name,
thy kingdom come,
thy will be done,
on earth as it is in heaven.

Give us this day our daily bread.
And forgive us our trespasses,
as we forgive those
who trespass against us.

And lead us not into temptation,
but deliver us from evil. Amen.

Padre Nuestro

Padre Nuestro, que estás en el cielo,
santificado sea tu nombre;

venga a nosotros tu reino;
hágase tu voluntad, en la tierra como en el cielo.
Danos hoy nuestro pan de cada día;
perdona nuestras ofensas,
como también nosotros perdonamos a los que nos ofenden;
no nos dejes caer en la tentación,
y líbranos del mal. Amén.

Dios te Salve, María

The next one we will cover is the Hail Mary, or in Spanish *Dios te Salve, María*—commonly just referred to as the *Dios te Salve*. "*Dios te salve, María*" translates to "God saves you, Mary," which is slightly different from the English translation, but overall the prayer is the same both in English and in Spanish. Much like the *Padre Nuestro*, the Hail Mary is an all-purpose prayer that can be brought out whenever you need help with anything from blessing to protection. The main difference is who you are speaking to. The Our Father connects you with God; the Hail Mary connects you to *La Virgen*. Either way, they'll be able to help, but some folks prefer to call on one over the other given their personal comfort levels with each spirit. The choice is ultimately yours.

Hail Mary

Hail Mary, Full of Grace,
The Lord is with thee.
Blessed art thou amongst women,
and blessed is the fruit of thy womb, Jesus Christ.
Holy Mary, Mother of God,
pray for us sinners now, and at the hour of death.
Amen.

Dios te Salve, María

Dios te salve, María, llena eres de gracia,
El Señor es contigo.
Bendita tú eres entre todas las mujeres,
y bendito es el fruto de tu vientre, Jesús.
Santa María, Madre de Dios,
ruega por nosotros, pecadores,
ahora y en la hora de nuestra muerte.
Amén.

Oración a San Miguel Arcangel

The third and final major prayer that comes in handy during this work is the prayer to St. Michael the Archangel. St. Michael, or *San Miguel*, is a powerful angel of protection who is called on to fend off evil spirits, protect from bodily harm, and cast out demons. In my experience he is friendly, humorous, and boundlessly energetic. The following prayer is said to evoke his presence.

St. Michael Prayer

St. Michael the Archangel, defend us in battle.
Be our defense against the wickedness and snares of the
    Devil.
May God rebuke him, we humbly pray, and do thou,
O prince of the heavenly hosts, by the power of God,
cast into hell Satan, and all the evil spirits
who prowl the world, seeking the ruin of souls. Amen.

Oración a San Miguel Arcángel

San Miguel Arcángel, defiéndenos en la lucha.
Se nuestro amparo contra la perversidad
* y acechanzas del demonio.*
Que Dios manifieste sobre el su poder,
es nuestra humilde suplica.
Y tú, oh Príncipe de la Milicia Celestial,
con el poder que Dios te ha conferido,
arroja al infierno a Príncipe, y a los demás espíritus
* malignos*
que vagan por el mundo para la perdición de las almas.
Amén.

The Holy Trinity

The last thing we'll touch on briefly is the simple translation of the Holy Trinity, otherwise known in English as "the Father, the Son, and the Holy Spirit." This comes up more than you'd think in this work, and I feel it's important to learn it in both English and Spanish—especially if the Spanish is intimidating for you and you'd like something smaller to begin with. To call upon the blessings of the Holy Trinity, simply make the sign of the cross over yourself—using your right hand touch your forehead, your solar plexus, your left shoulder, then your right shoulder in that order—or over an object—in the same up, down, left, right sequence—while saying, "In the name of the Father, and of the Son, and of the Holy Spirit," or in Spanish, "*En el nombre Del Padre, El Hijo, y El Espíritu Santo.*" This is done to imbue objects with holy power or to bring the protection of *El Espíritu Santo* over them.

Holy Medals

When I was growing up, I had a deep love of religious jewelry that developed early on. Like a lot of us, I was raised Catholic, and all the saints' medals and cross necklaces seemed so magical to me. The idea that they could turn away evil and protect against all manner of dangerous things was exciting! Fast-forward to present day and holy medals are my most favorite form of amulet. They're simple, durable, and made of metal, which is a good stout magically potent material. Better yet, they are cheap and easily found at most church stores or online.

When it comes to crafting a protective amulet, the actual symbol or type of pendant is largely up to you. It might be the medal of a particular saint, a devotional medal such as the Sacred Heart of Jesus or the Immaculate Heart of Mary, or even a cross. In Mexican American culture it's also common to see symbols such as *la Cruz de Caravaca* used as amulets of protection as well. If you are wanting to use a saint's medal, there are a few ways to go about choosing one. Pretty much all saints can lend you powers of protection, healing, blessing, and guidance. This means you can pick at random and come up with something good. Doing a little research on the saint may tell you something new and interesting! Some of them have really fascinating stories about battles with Satan and working great miracles, such as the story of St. Lucy. She became immovable. It was said that they hooked her up to a whole team of oxen but were unable to budge her from where she stood. That's pretty neat! You can also find the patron saint of your occupation. Basically every job you can think of from waiting tables to the military and even fishermen and writers all have patron saints. Same goes for hobbies: there are saints for archers, artists, musicians, and more! If you suffer from a particular illness, there's undoubtedly a saint that deals directly with that as well. They are a very versatile and inclusive class of spirits, and it's fun to get to know them through wearing their medals.

Whatever pendant you choose, you need to begin by cleansing it. I do this by running it under some ice-cold water. Spring water is ideal, but honestly, tap water will do just fine. The cold part is important; it cuts through any negativity and really energizes the medal. I pray while I do this, asking that the medal be purified. I then gently towel-dry the pendant, hold it in my hand, say the *Padre Nuestro* three times—unless it's a Mary-related medal, for which I say the *Dios te Salve* three times—and sprinkle holy water on it. This is enough for your everyday medals to repel evil and bring in good luck. If you're using a saint's medal, you may add a short prayer to the saint and ask them to bring you blessings and protection or anything else you may need.

For extra protection you may rub the pendant with protective herbs such as rosemary or rue. You can also make a tea of protective plants and dip the amulet into the mix and let it air-dry. If you feel that your amulet needs a charge or a power boost, you can leave it out under the full moon or in direct sunlight. You may also anoint it with special oils, bring it with you to mass, have a priest bless it, or go through the following ritual I developed to energize it further. If it begins to feel heavy or like its energy is dull, start over again from the cold-water cleanse. If the chain or pendant breaks, get rid of it and start over with a new one.

Amulet Blessing Ritual

If you'd like to energize your amulet or need to give it a power boost, start with a cleansed medal or pendant. Place the medal on a bay leaf in the center of three white candles arranged in a triangle, one candle for each character in the Holy Trinity

(Father, Son, Holy Spirit). Each candle should have a cross carved in it and be blessed with a *Padre Nuestro*. If you wish, you may dress the candles in holy oil, blessing oil, or an essential oil such as rosemary, eucalyptus, or camphor. In a pinch Vicks VapoRub is an excellent choice, and I'm not even joking. It contains both eucalyptus and camphor, which make for excellent high vibrational—borderline angelic—energy. Just a small dab to coat the candle is all you need. (Don't overdo it; it's flammable.) Sprinkle holy water on the medal and then say prayers to the saint depicted on the front. Or if you are using a cross or a Mary/Guadalupe medal, you can pray to God or *La Virgen* respectively. Burn the candles all the way down, and when they go out, your amulet will be fully loaded and ready to go.

St. Michael Pendant Ritual

St. Michael is a powerful protective spirit. He is most famous both for leading the army that defeated Lucifer and for casting him out of heaven. He is also said to be the "prince of heaven." His medals are the most protective, especially against demons, evil spirits, and misfortune.

To fix a St. Michael medal, begin by placing both the medal and the chain you intend to use in a shallow dish and covering it with holy water. Then set it aside. Take a cleansed red candle and carve a cross into the wax. Hold it and say the St. Michael prayer, asking him to protect you from all evil and misfortune. You may also anoint the candle with some kind of holy oil or St. Michael oil. You'll then light a charcoal disk and set it in a heat-safe container. These tend to smoke pretty bad at first, so I let them get hot either out on the porch or by an open window. While that's going, retrieve the chain and medal and gently towel them dry. Once the charcoal stops smoking and is glowing hot, light the candle and place some frankincense resin on the charcoal disk. Hold the medal in the smoke and say the *Padre Nuestro*. Then take the medal out of the smoke and pour some Florida Water onto it. Carefully take the medal by the chain—don't get your fingers involved here—and place it over the flame of the candle until it catches fire. Florida Water is alcohol-based and will burn much like rubbing alcohol. As it flames, say the St. Michael prayer (page 26) and ask that he protect you every moment you wear it. Once that's done and the flame has gone out, lay the chain and medal—careful, it's hot!—around the base of the candle and let it burn all the way down. You may wish to read Psalm 91 or recite the prayer to St. Michael once more while it finishes. Once the candle goes out, your medal is ready.

Psalm 91

He that dwelleth in the secret place of the most High shall abide under the shadow of the Almighty.

I will say of the Lord, He is my refuge and my fortress: my God; in him will I trust.

Surely he shall deliver thee from the snare of the fowler, and from the noisome pestilence.

He shall cover thee with his feathers, and under his wing shall thou trust: his truth shall be thy shield and buckler.

Thou shalt not be afraid for the terror by night; nor for the arrow that flieth by day;

Not for the pestilence that walketh in darkness; nor for the destruction that wasteth at noonday.

A thousand shall fall at thy side, and ten thousand at thy right hand; but it shall not come nigh thee.

Only with thine eyes shall thou behold and see the reward of the wicked.

Because thou hast made the Lord, which is my refuge, even
the most High, thy habitation;

There shall no evil befall thee, neither shall any plague come
nigh thy dwelling.

For he shall give his angels charge over thee, to keep thee in
all thy ways.

They shall bear thee up in their hands, lest thou dash thy
foot against a stone.

Thou shalt tread upon the lion and adder: the young lion
and the dragon shalt thou trample under feet.

Because he hath set his love upon me, therefore will I
deliver him: I will set him on high, because he hath
known my name.

He shall call upon me, and I will answer him: I will be with
him in trouble; I will deliver him, and honour him.

With long life will I satisfy him, and show him my salvation.

3

La Virgen

In Mexican culture we do things a little differently, and religion is no exception. Though the church has tried for centuries to get us to behave, we have always had a particular affinity for seeing between the lines, diving deep into the many mysteries and coming back with something most people would call "magic." Most of us claim to be good Catholics and for most folks that is correct. Still, others reject Catholicism and will instead call themselves *Guadalupanos* or people who follow the teaching and veneration of *La Virgen de Guadalupe,* or simply Guadalupe for short. This is a unique spirit known by many names: Virgin Mary, Queen of Heaven, Mother of God, *La Madonna*, and Tonantzin. She is our protector, our savior, and our queen. It's not uncommon in Mexican culture for folks to nearly completely leave out God and Jesus and work solely with our Heavenly Mother Guadalupe. After all, she's much more forgiving than God and is believed to wear the pants in their relationship—what she says goes. She is capable of bestowing a great number of blessings and favors upon those who seek her intercession, and many folks will run to *La Virgen* the way that children run to their mother for protection.

Some folks will become furious and tell you that Guadalupe is not Mary in any way, shape, or form, but a simple glance at the image is enough to tell you it's Marian in nature. The spirit world is full of paradoxes and sometimes two spirits are the same and separate all at once. The spirit known as Mary is made up of many different faces. She is a complicated being and there are many things that folks misunderstand about her. The first is that they believe she is too soft and docile to provide much protection. Believing this, however, is a mistake. There are a great many depictions of her beating the devil to a pulp with either her bare hands or on occasion a club or spear. Those who are under her protection know just how fierce a mother's love can be. Even during exorcisms it's been noted that demons struggle and cry out when presented with the name of Jesus, but will show outright terror when the priest calls in Mary. More than that, all forms of Mary can offer magical power related to healing, blessings, fertility, and love. She is also the doorway to the other higher powers; some of her titles like "Queen of Heaven," "Mother of God," and "Mother of Angels" suggest she is in charge, which means that if the saints, angels, and other holy spirits are on the same team, she is the coach. Through her we gain access to all the powers that heaven has to offer. These special titles and abilities extend to her form as *La Virgen de Guadalupe.*

Guadalupe is a unique creature that is half Mary and half Aztec mother goddess known as Tonantzin. As such this particular spirit has some special attributes. First, she is the most primal of all the Marys. With her Aztec roots, she's what we call *más chingona* and will pull up with a razor-sharp machete anytime you need to deal with enemies. She will also tenderly bestow new love upon you, as well as healing, divine guidance, and open roads. Guadalupe may be called on for all manner of things, so never hesitate to seek her intercession. It is said that no one who has ever come to her for help was left unaided. As we go through this chapter you will come to realize that this spirit is much older and bigger than just "Mary, Mother of God" or Tonantzin, she's a representation of the divine feminine, which mean that her roots stretch back to ancient times. She's very old, and she's very powerful. When we pray to Guadalupe, we are summoning a goddess from the heart of the earth and the highest tier of heaven.

The Story of Cuauhtlatoatzin

The story of Cuauhtlatoatzin (kwa-oot-la-tow-at-zeen) is the most important thing to learn about Coatlaxopeuh (Guadalupe). It chronicles her first four apparitions on earth and details her most widely known miracle, which can be seen to this day in Mexico City. This narrative is popularly known as the story of Juan Diego. Juan Diego is the Christian/Spanish name of Cuauhtlatoatzin, but out of respect for him and his culture, I will be referring to him by his indigenous name as I tell this tale . . .

Picture it: Mount Tepeyac, just outside of what is now Mexico City. It's December 9, 1531, and Cuauhtlatoatzin is walking over the hill, allegedly on his way to mass. As he reached the top of the hill, he began to hear the most beautiful singing he had ever experienced. He followed the voice and found a beautiful indigenous woman surrounded in golden light. She spoke his native tongue and told him that she was the Holy Mother. She asked him to go to the bishop and tell him that she wanted a temple built on that very hill. The same hill was once sacred to the Aztec earth goddess—who bore a striking resemblance to the apparition before him. She told him that she wanted the temple built there so that her people would have a place to pray to her and she could help ease their distress.

Accepting her mission, he ran to town and told the bishop what he had seen and what the woman had told him. The bishop didn't believe him and turned him away. He returned to the spot on the hill, and she appeared again. He told her what had happened and how he felt he had failed. He tried to explain to her that people weren't going to listen to someone like him: an indigenous person of very little standing. Still, she insisted that he was the one she wanted to carry out the task. So the next morning (December 10) he went again to the bishop. This time the bishop told him that he would do what she asked, but only if there was a sign. Cuauhtlatoatzin returned to the mountain once more and told her of the bishop's request. She agreed and promised to offer a sign the next day (December 11) and asked him to return then.

Meanwhile Cuauhtlatoatzin's uncle had become very sick and was quickly nearing the end of his life. Because of this, Cuauhtlatoatzin was unable to return to the hill and chose to stay by his uncle's side instead. The next day, December 12, it became clear this was the end for his uncle, so Cuauhtlatoatzin set out to find a priest to give last rites. Ashamed of breaking his promise, he tried to go around the hill instead of over it so he wouldn't have to face the woman. On the road she appeared to him once more and asked him why he had not come as instructed. He explained about his uncle, and this is when she spoke the famous words: "¿No estoy yo aquí, que soy tu madre?" ("Am I not here, I who am your mother?") She then assured him that his uncle was healed and instructed him to go to the top of the hill, gather the flowers he would find there, and bring them to her. He was confused: It was December and there was snow on the hill. No flowers would be growing for months. Still, he did as she asked and climbed the hill. There, in the dead of winter, grew beautiful roses. He gathered them into the front of his tilma (a garment a bit like a poncho) and took them back down to the road. It was then that something peculiar happened. It's said that she took the flowers into her arms and then promptly gave them back to him, instructing that he go to town but keep the flowers a secret and show no one but the bishop.

So he wrapped the roses in the front of his tilma and did as she asked. When he got to the office, the bishop's men made him wait outside for several hours. During that time the men became curious about what he was holding. Whatever it was smelled wonderful and they wanted a peek, but Cuauhtlatoatzin would not show them. Around the edges they could catch glimpses of beautiful fresh flowers, but when they'd reach to try and touch them, they were just paint on the fabric. When they'd pull their hand back, they were real flowers again. Finally he was allowed into the bishop's office where he came up to the desk and opened the tilma to reveal the roses. To all of their astonishment, an image of the woman was emblazoned on the front of the tilma—thus surprising all of them with the requested sign.

Later, his uncle told the story of the fourth apparition that appeared at his bedside. She healed him and told him that she wished to be known as Coatlaxopeuh (pronounced "Kwat-luh-show-pay" and roughly translated by some as "She who crushes the serpent" or "She who has dominion over serpents"). It's suggested that we got her current name Guadalupe due to a slight miscommunication. You see, the Spanish already had a black Madonna figure in Spain known as Guadalupe—which sounds an awful lot like Coatlaxopeuh—and they assumed that's what the indigenous man meant and that the two figures were one and the same.

Cuauhtlatoatzin, popularly known as Juan Diego, became the first indigenous saint from the Americas. That tilma is still intact to this day, and it holds many mysteries. It's on display in Mexico City at the Basilica of Our Lady of Guadalupe. Above the doors are written the words "¿No estoy yo aquí, que soy tu madre?"

The Symbols and Mysteries of Coatlaxopeuh

Since 1531, the tilma with her image has been studied profusely with some startling results. Some of these stories are hard to verify, but they can be found far and wide and have been included in many books and documentaries about this mysterious image. First of all, it has survived its nearly five hundred years here on earth, which is remarkable. It is made from cactus fiber, which should have decomposed within several years. Yet it's in remarkably good shape and has suffered no fading or cracking. The image is incredibly crisp to the point of being able to see small veins and shapes in the eyes. People who have studied the eyes in depth have noticed in their reflection you can clearly see the image of Cuauhtlatoatzin showing the bishop and his men the roses and consequently the image of *La Virgen*. These extremely small details require the use of modern technology to even be able to see them, let alone paint them by hand in 1531. If that's not proof enough of the miraculousness of this object, through the use of infrared photography, studies have been able to show that there is no underdrawing—something that would be necessary in order to paint a portrait in such exacting detail. This further reinforces the idea that the image was not made by human hands. It's also said that depending on which direction

you look at the image, she can seem either European or indigenous, symbolizing the unity of the people.

Other strange things are present in the more immediate sym-
bolism. The image contains many native cultural symbols, such
as her black sash symbolizing her pregnancy. This meant that she
was specifically showing herself as a native woman, not simply
a dark Madonna but an indigenous woman from the Americas.
But even stranger is the fact that the stars on her mantle match
the pattern of the stars that would have hung over Mount
Tepeyac on that same day. Stranger still, the layout of the stars is
in reverse, suggesting they are being viewed from the other side
of our normal perspective. They are shown as if you are looking
down toward the earth from the heavens. Think that's weird?
Hold on to your hat. The tilma is said to maintain a constant
heat of 98.6 degrees Fahrenheit—the exact temperature of the
human body.

The tilma has survived many years, many disasters, and many
attempts to debunk its authenticity. She has remained intact and
can still be seen today in Mexico City. You can find several books
and documentaries on its seemingly endless mysteries and symbols. To this day it's one of the most powerful Christian miracles
and truly evidence of the divine mother here on earth.

The Implications of Coatlaxopeuh

Though the Catholic Spaniards understood the apparition as little
more than proof their religion was superior, it was said the indigenous people took much more than that from her symbols. Most
don't know this but a very similar figure of a young indigenous
woman who bore a striking resemblance to the one we now call
La Virgen had already been appearing to the natives for many

years. At the time of her miracle, the people of Mexico were being forced to relinquish their Aztec gods. This wasn't something they did willingly, and many were murdered during the years of conversion. This was a bloody and terrible time for the indigenous population, and they were desperate to find a way to hold on to the life they had always known while still assimilating into this new world order. When Coatlaxopeuh/Guadalupe appeared, it was the sign they had been seeking. You see, she was one of them with her powerful Aztec symbols. She bore a striking resemblance to a mother goddess known to them as Tonantzin. The fact that the Spaniards recognized her as their own meant they were willing to let the local populace worship her. It was through Coatlaxopeuh/Guadalupe that they were able to find some common ground and got to secretly retain some of their Aztec traditions.

As we move forward, we must understand the goddess Tonantzin. This powerful spirit is complex, and a lot was lost during the conversion, so coming to understand her finer points has been a struggle. I contacted PhDs and shamans alike trying to fully get her into focus, but even they seemed stumped by her mysteries. In my research I've found that Tonantzin is both a goddess and a title. She is the mighty "Mother Earth" spirit of the Aztecs, and her image is strikingly similar to that of Guadalupe's apparition. Her spirit provides us with sacred foods like corn and plants for our remedies. She is powerful and encompasses all of the mother goddesses, including many seen as both creators and destroyers. Due to this, Tonantzin is also a title that means "revered mother" applied to all worthy motherly goddesses. The apparition of Guadalupe, for instance, became known as Tonantzin Coatlaxopeuh. Think of it like "Our Lady": they are all Mary in theory, but Our Lady of Sorrows and Our Lady of Lourdes carry very different energies even if they are technically the faces of the same divine mother spirit. There's a lot of overlap in this idea between Christianity and the Aztecs. In other schools of magic Hekate works very similarly, but we won't get into that here. We'll just say that it is not uncommon for mother goddesses around the world to act a bit like Russian nesting dolls where one mighty spirit contains multitudes.

It was said that the indigenous people noticed several key things about the image. First, she was indigenous herself: she was one of them, spoke their language, and specifically chose to appear to one of their people. Second, the golden light behind her was understood to be the sun. The fact that she was standing in front of it, blocking it out, was taken as a symbol that she was more powerful than their sun god Huitzilopochtli. The fact that she was standing on the moon meant she was more powerful than their lunar god Tezcatlipoca. Now understand that these ideas were recorded by Catholic friars who undoubtedly added their own twist. They said that these signs indicated to the indigenous population that Catholicism was more powerful than the Aztec religions. However, I have often seen these symbols as her being a spirit that encompassed the other Aztec gods or was backed by Huitzilopochtli and supported by Tezcatlipoca, who were both powerful gods. No matter how you interpret it, it was clear that Guadalupe/Coatlaxopeuh showed up right when she was needed the most, and she assumed an identity that would allow the indigenous population to sneak their beliefs and spirits by their oppressors and continue to worship the old gods in a new way. We must never forget these roots as we work with her.

Furthermore, there's something very interesting in the Bible that sounds an awful lot like Guadalupe. You see in Revelation 12 there is a very odd passage about "a great wonder in heaven, a woman clothed with the sun, and the moon under her feet." It also mentions her being crowned in stars and pregnant, two other symbols that match Guadalupe. In the passage from Revelation the woman is about to give birth and faces off against a great dragon with many heads. Weird, right? Well, hold on while I get out the red string and conspiracy theory map. Take a look at the dates and numbers. First of all, remember it's Revelation 12, and the apparitions came to a climax on December 12, or 12/12. In numerology it's common to add the numbers together, which means that 12 (1 + 2) comes out to 3, which is a widely known holy number throughout many different faiths. Revelation is also the sixty-sixth book of the Bible (6 + 6 = 12, 1 + 2 = 3). The date she arrived was December 9, or 12/9 which adds up to 12 (1 + 2 + 9 = 12), and then 12 makes 3 once more. Note that arriving on the date of 9 makes for three 3s (3 + 3 + 3 = 9). I'm not saying that it means anything, but it certainly is a curious anomaly.

No matter how you decide to process all the symbols, history, and information surrounding the holy spirit that is Guadalupe, it's clear that she is a powerful cross-cultural symbol of the divine feminine. With her Aztec roots she is the fiercest of the Marys and not opposed to primal warfare when needed, especially when it comes to protecting her children. She is a goddess, and she made a promise to her people that whoever should call out to her in their time of need would receive her aid.

Setting Up a Guadalupe Altar

To begin working with Guadalupe it's a nice idea to make an altar. There are many ways to go about this, but I will cover some basics here and I encourage you to make it your own. Altars are very personal and should reflect not only the subject but also your relationship with this spirit. This is the space where you will be burning your novenas, saying your prayers, and working your *hechizos*.

Every altar needs four main things: an image of Guadalupe, flame, water, and smoke. We'll get into each of these a little later, but let's start from scratch with the working surface.

You'll want to find a place where you can set up your items and they won't be disturbed. It doesn't have to be fancy. It can be a shelf or the top of a dresser—whatever you have is fine. Begin by cleaning the space: the entire room itself should be cleaned and put into order. Not only does this help the energy of the room, but we have to remember this might be the first time she's brought to your home, and first impressions are important. The surface you'll be building the altar on should be cleansed energetically as well. This can be done a bunch of ways, so pick your favorite. I like to do this by spraying the surface down with a mix of Florida Water and holy water and then wiping it dry with a white cloth. You can also cover the surface with white flower petals and then sweep them off to purify it. If you'd like to anoint the space with holy oils, you can do so as well. Remember this process should reflect your personal style and there's no one specific way. I also recommend burning purifying incense to get the space cleared and ready for her arrival. Be sure to open the windows when you do this. For more tips and tricks on cleansing a space, see the chapter on *limpias.*

Once the area is set up, you can lay down a nice altar cloth if you want, but it's not necessary. You'll then get your image of Guadalupe. It can be a statue—which is what I prefer—or a framed photo of her image will do nicely as well. It doesn't have to be fancy: you can print out a picture online and put it in a dollar store frame—that's totally fine. Always work with what you have access to. Whatever you choose, you'll want to cleanse the image. If you are using a picture frame, you can simply wipe it down with a Florida Water solution or some holy water, like you did the surface of the altar, or waft it through some cleansing smoke. If you have a statue though, you may want to give it a bath, which helps cleanse and purify the vessel, and bless it with holy power. To do this, I combine about three cups holy water, the juice of one lime, and fresh rue in a white or glass bowl. I mix the ingredients in by hand while praying. Once it's all set, I place the statue in the bowl and use a white cloth to squeeze the liquid over the top of it until it's been totally saturated. I then take the damp cloth to it and get any dirt off that might be present and gently towel it dry. I usually end by saying a prayer over the statue. In this case I would say three Hail Marys. It's important to do this once a year to refresh the statue and keep it a clear open channel for her. Once that's done, you're ready to set it on your altar. Be sure to take into account what your statue is made from and what kind of base it has before submerging it in water. If in doubt, cleanse it with frankincense or copal smoke instead.

The second thing you'll need is flame. A candle acts as both an offering of light and energy to the spirit and a beacon to attract their attention. So when the candle is lit, she is listening, and when I snuff the candle, I say goodbye and she goes—but never too far. For most of my spirits I prefer a novena that I light and snuff as needed, but for Guadalupe I like to place two white stick candles on either side of her statue. I have a thing about symmetry, and I like the look of this the best. But any candle arrangement you prefer will do just fine. I like to use plain white unscented candles for this, and I carve crosses into them and anoint them with holy oils. This sets a nice spiritual tone for the altar.

You will also need a glass vessel for water offerings. Water is a powerful spiritual element. The offering of cool water does several things. It's refreshing and purifying for the spirits, and it acts like a filter for the energy of the space. Also, water is an excellent conductor of spiritual energy, so it functions a bit like a lightning rod for the spirit's presence. Furthermore, the surface of the water creates a liminal space where air and water meet, which generates a small portal or window through which they may interact with our world. For Guadalupe, I often add a splash of rose water to her offering glass because of her affinity for roses. The water should be changed at least once a week—more if your cat likes to drink out of it or you find bugs in it—and should always be served cool.

The last thing your altar needs is smoke. Smoke acts as an offering that is pleasing to the spirits, and it helps to carry our prayers up to heaven. It can also work to keep the space energetically pure. The type of incense you choose can also influence your requests. For instance, if you are saying prayers and asking her to open a road, using an unblocking or road-opening incense will help get that message to her. Or if you are asking for love, using a romantic-smelling incense will help. Generally for Guadalupe I burn floral or rose-scented incense sticks, along with copal and frankincense on special occasions.

Other options for offerings can be candles burned in her name, apples, coffee, flowers, perfume, songs sung, honey, *y más*. Be sure to keep the altar clean and organized. Remove any perishable offerings such as food or flowers from the altar in a timely fashion. Messy altars with moldy offerings attract bad spirits. So be sure to keep the space clean both physically and energetically to avoid any unsavory interactions with the other side. Spent offerings can be thrown in the trash when you are done with them.

Now that you've completed your altar you are ready to begin working with her. Remember that Guadalupe is the gateway to the other holy spirits so her altar may also be used as a home for saint statues, and you may burn your *velas* and work your *hechizos* here in her space, or pray to God or Jesus as necessary.

Apart from what I've mentioned here, anything else you add or don't add to the altar is largely up to you. You may add crystals or holy items; you may add charms and talismans. I like to place a rosary especially dedicated to her on the altar and use it when I pray to her. The rosary is a powerful prayer system for working with all forms of Mary, including Guadalupe. We'll discuss that in a moment.

Guadalupe's Machete

One of the things you can do with your patron spirits is arm them with weapons. Throughout history Mary has favored weapons such as the club wielded by *La Madonna del Soccorso*. For Guadalupe, I've always felt that a machete is her weapon of choice and have given her one to use. I recommend that you do the same when you feel it is appropriate. I was able to find a wide selection of blades online that were not too big and very affordable. Once you have the machete, cleanse it and bless it by carefully washing the blade in holy water and anointing it with your choice of oils. I also recommend decorating the handle as an act of devotion.

Once the blade is prepared and ready, present it to her in a short ritual of your own making. As you offer it to her, ask that she use it to slice through any bindings that hold you back, cut down any enemies that wish you harm, and clear a path ahead of you to your goals. By arming Guadalupe you are forging a deeper connection and expanding her role in your life in a meaningful way. This simple act can have a very powerful response. You may also give her items like a hammer to defend you but also to help you build the life you want. Giving gifts like this should be a sign of gratitude *after* forming a meaningful relationship with her.

Praying the Rosary

The rosary is prayed for many, many reasons. First, it helps us honor Mary/Guadalupe and brings us closer to the Mother of God.

This act of devotion lets her know we are serious about working with her. The rosary is not a quick or simple task. It takes some time to go through all the steps, and this dedication gets noticed by both her and God. In some schools of thought, praying the rosary earns you a certain amount of "points" that can be cashed in for certain favors. For instance, when someone dies, it's common for groups to gather to pray the rosary as a way to work off some of the deceased person's spiritual debt and ease their transition into heaven. The prayers seem to open the road to where they need to go. Like all forms of prayer, it brings the divine closer to us, affording us more of their attention, protection, and blessings. It also affords us an opportunity to ask for favors and prove that we are willing to put in some work to pay for the favor.

We must also remember that Mary is simply the earthly human face of a much larger spirit. When we pray the rosary, we are actually forging a connection with the divine feminine—she who birthed everything. I encourage you to look much deeper at this process, beyond just praying some Christian prayers to a Christian woman. You are connecting to the first mother and honoring the power of her spirit. In this way, we make sure she is not forgotten.

As you'll see momentarily, the rosary is quite repetitive and requires you to say the *Dios te Salve* over fifty times, along with several other prayers that must be memorized in order to accomplish the entire thing. This can be very tricky—even downright frustrating at first—but after a while it becomes much easier. The repetition of prayers, when done correctly, induces a meditative trancelike state, where you may receive visions or messages from the divine or otherwise feel connected. The groups of ten beads are known as *decades*. Each prayer is marked by a single bead, and occasionally a space between beads, going clockwise as follows . . .

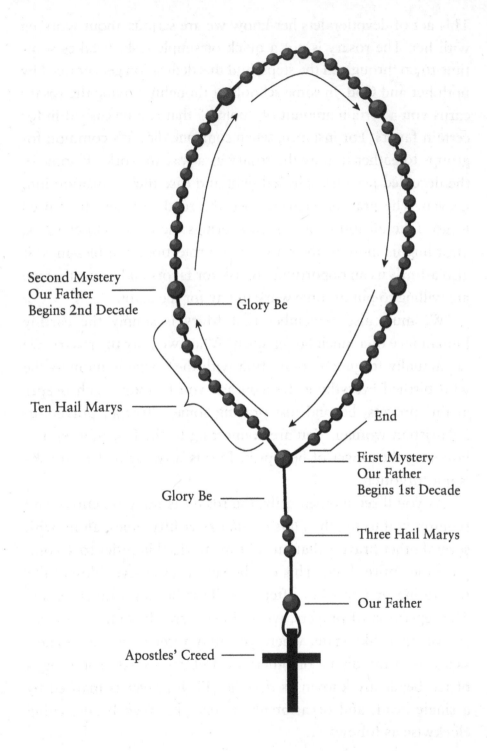

Second Mystery
Our Father
Begins 2nd Decade

Glory Be

Ten Hail Marys

End

First Mystery
Our Father
Begins 1st Decade

Glory Be

Three Hail Marys

Our Father

Apostles' Creed

You've already learned the Our Father and the Hail Mary in previous chapters; here we will learn the Apostles' Creed, the Glory Be, and the Hail Holy Queen prayed at the completion of the rosary. The Apostles' Creed is often left out by those who are approaching this work from outside mainstream Catholicism and you may substitute a meaningful prayer of your own. Just remember that all the standard prayers hold power and do have their place in this work. While it may sound a little "culty" in places, this prayer calls upon many holy figures and events in the Bible to draw up strength.

Apostles' Creed

I believe in God,
the Father Almighty,
Creator of heaven and earth,
and in Jesus Christ, His only Son, our Lord,
who was conceived by the Holy Spirit,
born of the Virgin Mary,
suffered under Pontius Pilate,
was crucified, died, and was buried;
He descended into hell;
on the third day He rose again from the dead;
He ascended into heaven,
and is seated at the right hand of God the Father Almighty;
from there He will come to judge the living and the dead.
I believe in the Holy Spirit,
the Holy Catholic Church,
the communion of Saints,
the forgiveness of sins,
the resurrection of the body,
and life everlasting.
Amen.

El Credo

*Creo en Dios, Padre todopoderoso, creador del Cielo y
    de la Tierra.*
Creo en Jesucristo su único Hijo, Nuestro Señor,
que fue concebido por obra y gracia del Espíritu Santo;
nació de Santa María Virgen;
padeció bajo el poder de Poncio Pilato;
fue crucificado, muerto y sepultado;
descendió a los infiernos;
al tercer día resucitó de entre los muertos;
subió a los cielos y está a la diestra de Dios Padre;
desde allí ha de venir a juzgar a los vivos y a los muertos.
Creo en el Espíritu Santo, en la Santa Iglesia Católica,
la comunión de los Santos en el perdón de los pecados
la resurrección de los muertos y la vida eterna.
Amén.

Glory Be

Glory be to the Father and to the Son and to the Holy Spirit.
As it was in the beginning, is now, and ever shall be,
world without end. Amen.

Gloria

Gloria al Padre, al Hijo y al Espíritu Santo.
Como era en el principio, ahora y siempre,
por los siglos de los siglos.
Amén.

Hail, Holy Queen

Hail, holy Queen, Mother of mercy,
hail, our life, our sweetness, and our hope.
To thee do we cry, poor banished children of Eve:
to thee do we send up our sighs,
mourning and weeping in this vale of tears.
Turn then, most gracious Advocate,
thine eyes of mercy toward us,
and after this our exile,
show unto us the blessed fruit of thy womb,
Jesus, O merciful, O loving, O sweet Virgin Mary! Amen.

Salve Regina

Dios te salve, Reina y Madre de misericordia,
vida, dulzura, y esperanza nuestra, Dios te salve.
A ti clamamos los desterrados hijos de Eva.
A ti suspiramos gimiendo y llorando en este valle de lágrimas.
Ea, pues, Señora, abogada nuestra:
vuelve a nosotros esos tus ojos misericordiosos.
Y después de este destierro, muéstranos a Jesús, fruto
*   bendito de tu vientre.*
Oh clemente, oh piadosa, oh dulce Virgen María. Ruega por
*   nosotros,*
Santa Madre de Dios, para que seamos dignos de las
*   promesas de Cristo. Amén.*

The Mysteries

You may have noticed that there are spaces along the rosary in which you are supposed to pause and meditate on certain "mysteries." These are important events in the life of Christ to remember and think about when saying these prayers. The four categories of mystery group different parts of his timeline into the Joyful Mysteries, Luminous Mysteries, Sorrowful Mysteries, and Glorious Mysteries. When praying the rosary, we choose one category to work with. Each category contains five events or "mysteries" that impart some sort of lesson or "fruit." So you may choose to pray the rosary and go through each of the five Luminous Mysteries one day and the next go through the Sorrowful Mysteries. Some folks choose based on the day of the week; others choose which mysteries to pray for depending on what they are needing that day. It's up to you.

For the purposes of this book, however, I would like to present something a little different. While you are welcome to look up and pray the traditional mysteries—which I highly encourage—I would like to share with you a personal devotion that I have created myself and use when praying to Guadalupe. I call these the "Guadalupano Mysteries," and they detail five important events ("mysteries") and their symbolic meanings ("fruit"). These might be a little easier to work with for those who may not be completely ready to embrace Catholic practices but wish to work with Guadalupe.

The First Appearance

The first mystery is Guadalupe's first appearance on Mount Tepeyac, when she proclaims that she would like a temple built on that spot so that her people can ask her for help and she can assist them. This mystery shows that she wants us to turn to her for all of our needs and that she wants to provide for us.

The Second Appearance

The second mystery is Guadalupe's second appearance when she insists that she wants Cuauhtlatoatzin, an indigenous person of no standing in Spanish Mexico, to be her chosen messenger. This mystery shows that she is on the side of the oppressed and the marginalized. She will always favor the underdog.

The Third Appearance

The third mystery of Guadalupe is her third appearance, when she utters those famous words: "¿No estoy yo aquí, que soy tu madre?" This is a very special moment in the story when she declares that she's not just the Mother of God, but our mother too. More than that, she seems offended when we don't trust her to handle our problems. She wants us to turn to her like a mother and confide our deepest wishes and secrets. She will guide and protect us and be there for us always.

The Miracle of the Roses

The fourth mystery is the Miracle of the Roses, or the moment when Cuauhtlatoatzin presents the flowers and discovers the image of Guadalupe on his tilma. Even though he had no reason to believe the flowers were growing in the dead of winter, he still followed through and was rewarded with arguably the most powerful Marian miracle of all time. In order to make this happen he had to have enough faith to follow her instructions. This mystery proves that we will be rewarded for our faith in her and that she will help us in surprising ways if we can only follow her direction.

The Fifth Appearance

The fifth and final mystery of Guadalupe is when she appears to Cuauhtlatoatzin's uncle and heals him. This event shows that she keeps her promises and can set things right even when we fear they are too far gone.

I encourage you to work with these mysteries when getting to know the rosary and this complex spirit. You may find deeper meanings or "fruit" from these mysteries, and that's what makes them so powerful. What do these events say to you about the spirit we call Guadalupe? Take time with each and let her teach you about herself.

The Seven Sorrows

Apart from the above mentioned mysteries, you will also find there are different kinds of rosaries including those dedicated to *La Dolorosa* or Our Lady of Sorrows. This rosary is dedicated to a very particular Marian devotion known as the Seven Sorrows of Mary. If you wish to dive deeper into Marian devotion, I highly recommend going there next after learning to pray the standard rosary. *La Dolorosa* is a fearsome and powerful dark aspect of Mary. She is incredibly protective and teaches us that through suffering we may appreciate the beauty of life.

Rosary Magic

Praying the rosary is incredibly powerful. Not only is it connecting us with Mary/Guadalupe, but through her, it connects us with Jesus and God. This brings us into communion with not only one, but three major spirits in heaven all at once. Mary/Guadalupe isn't just a powerful spirit herself, but also a door to the others. As "Queen of Heaven" and "Mother of Angels" she can be a gateway to all the saints and the angels as well. We can connect to them through her while praying the rosary. Beyond focusing the power of prayer, the rosary itself may become a useful tool in the everyday life of a folk magician.

In mainstream Catholic teaching they explain that the rosary itself holds no power, it is simply a string of beads with no innate mystical properties. While this may be true to some extent, as spiritual workers we know that all things collect energy as time goes on. When you pray the rosary repeatedly and hold it in your hands as you connect with the divine, that energy gets absorbed into the rosary. The power of all your prayers stored within one vessel makes for a very potent tool. As such, you may use your rosary to ward off bad energies and devils, protect yourself from malicious witchcraft, and call the divine at the drop of a hat. This is why heirloom rosaries can be extremely powerful: they carry the prayers of our ancestors as well as our own.

If you wish to use a rosary as a holy talisman or amulet, you'll want to begin with either a rosary that once belonged to a beloved family member or a new rosary. I don't like to use rosaries from folks I don't know without cleansing them first. If you've purchased a vintage rosary, cleanse it by sprinkling it with holy water and salt. If you plan to use it as an amulet or talisman instead of just for prayer, you'll want to dedicate it to its intended purpose with a prayer. (For example: "I pray that this rosary keep my vehicle safe from all harm.") Then, hold it firmly and pray the *Dios te Salve* three times. It is now ready to be placed wherever you need the protection and light of *La Virgen* or *El Espíritu Santo*. I put one in my car and carry one with me when I'm going into a haunted house. Remember to use your rosaries for prayer regularly so they continue to keep their power.

Though every rosary is most effective while being used in prayer, they can be a helpful addition to regular spellwork. Some rosaries are made of precious stones, sturdy metals, or natural wood. Each kind may contribute different properties or energies to the work.

For love, pray with a rosary dedicated to St. Anne. For protection, pray with a St. Michael rosary. Red rosaries for power and wood beads for peace. To protect your novena or spell, place a rosary around it. This keeps away bad spirits and other outside influences. Rosaries can be placed around haunted objects to keep them quiet and hung in doorways to keep out evil. To stop a mirror from being used as a portal for evil, hang a well-used rosary on it. If a person is afflicted with a spiritual ailment you may place a St. Benedict rosary around their neck. Just don't forget, in serious situations you'll always be better off actively using it than placing it somewhere. This is not necessarily a traditional Mexican practice, but it's one you see regularly in the states.

Four-Rosary Spell for Protection

This spell is designed to protect your home from evil by entangling *El Diablo* in your prayers every time he or any of his minions attempts to come close.

You'll need:

4 rosaries all used at least once
1 white candle
Holy water

Begin by gathering all four rosaries into your hands and praying the *Dios te Salve* three times. Take the white candle, carve the sign of the cross into it, and pray the *Dios te Salve* over it. Affix it to a plate or set it in a candleholder and light it. Gather the rosaries together around the base of the candle and sprinkle them with holy water, praying the *Dios te Salve* over them. Once the candle has burned down, take the rosaries and hang them in the four corners of your home with a prayer. Once a month repeat this ritual to keep them active and working.

Our Lady of Sorrows Protection Spell

Guadalupe, as a face of Mary, has been through more than most of us can imagine in a lifetime. This includes watching her children brutally tortured and then murdered in front of her. This aspect of her—the one who has suffered—is extremely protective. She had to go through it once, and that was plenty for her. She will stop at nothing to protect her remaining children. This is a spell to create a rosary of protection that can be used in many ways. You'll want either a "Seven Sorrows" rosary, a rosary with black beads, or an Our Lady of Sorrows chaplet. I recommend doing this at her altar while burning incense to her as an offering.

You'll need:

1 black candle
1 bowl (glass or white bowls are preferred, but use what you have)
Holy water
1 rosary of your choosing

Carve a cross into the candle on one side and the words "Defend us Holy Mother" on the other side. Hold the candle while praying the *Dios te Salve*, as well as a prayer for protection. You may also anoint it with a protective oil if you'd like. Affix the candle to the bottom of the bowl and fill it with holy water. Make sure it's the water is at least an inch deep. Light the candle, and begin praying the *Dios te Salve* while taking the rosary and placing it down over the candle and into the bowl so that the candle is in the center. When you finish praying the *Dios te Salve*, continue praying by asking that she defend and protect you and your family in every instance of your life. Ask that she watch over you and, turn away all evil, and save you from any attack or misfortune like that which befell her son Jesus Christ. Ask that we be saved from the thorns and that they be turned outward toward our enemies so that we may remain safe and unharmed. As you do this, you may dip your fingers into the water and flick the drops around your room or home to cleanse it of all evil. End your prayers with one more recitation of the *Dios te Salve*. Leave it the rosary there in the water until the candle burns all the way out.

Once the candle has burned down, you may remove the rosary and let it dry on your altar. After it is dry, you may carry it with you or hang it in your home or on your front door for protection. You may also place it around photos of loved ones when they need protection from evil and harm. Do so with prayer and reverence.

4

Las Velas

Another favorite tool in American Brujeria is *las velas*. Candles small and tall are used in our rituals, but the most representative of our traditions is the novena candle. Novena candles have roots in Roman funeral tradition but have evolved over the years to signify an act of faith when facing a great number of situations and obstacles. These candles, found frequently in religious stores and small *tiendas* in cities with dense Latinx populations, are burned as a means of sending up a beacon to the divine. Some are used to call upon specific saints; others are lit for individual purposes such as love, luck, prosperity, and protection. Though their purposes may be different, they are often handled the same way.

The word *novena* means "nine," and it's often said that these candles are meant to burn for nine days in a row. You may also find them called seven-day candles for the same reason. However, it's very rare that they burn for a full seven to nine days. Usually they will only last three to six days, sometimes more or less depending on the state of the flame—which we'll talk about later. Whether it's three days or nine days, the point to notice is that this is magic worked over several days. When doing such a spell, we are reinforcing it over and over again. Like the burning of the candle, results from novena work are often thorough and long-lasting. This is different from a usual candle spell, which will burn for only one day and have quick but short-lived results. Though both have their pros and cons, I find a novena may be burned to adequately address just about any situation.

So how does it work? First, we have to understand that all things pick up or record the energies that they come in contact with. Soft materials like fabric pick up energy very easily but also lose it quickly. Conversely, hard materials like metal don't pick up energy as easily, but they hold on to it for a lot longer once they do. Wax is a perfect in between, both soft enough to readily pick up energy and hard enough to hold on to it while the candle burns. We can use this to our advantage by placing our intention, energy, and prayer into our candle wax. As we burn it our intentions and prayers are drawn up into the wick and fed to the activating element of fire, which transmutes our intention to light, heat, and energy that radiate out from our candle. This becomes a beacon for spirit. It's a little like sending up a supernatural Bat-Signal for God, the angels, and the saints to see and respond to. As we go along, you'll see that fixing a novena is very much like writing a secret message in herbs and oils that only the divine can decipher. The spirit of your candle is a bit like a messenger pigeon that can fly to the other side on our behalf and deliver our message.

The key to working with novenas is faith. As with most forms of magic, if you are pessimistic about your results or refuse to believe at all, *they won't work*. Faith is the power they thrive off of, and when paired with daily ritual, novenas can be extremely powerful. The idea with the novenas is that you return to them every day and work them. It doesn't have to take much time—you don't have to spend hours or start over every day—but taking a moment each day one's burning reinforces your intention. Say some prayers—particularly the *Dios te Salve* if you are burning them at your Guadalupe altar—and renew your belief in their power. With these simple acts of faith and devotion to our cause, these ordinary candles become extraordinary allies that support us along our path.

Saints or Intentions?

Early on, almost all novena candles were for specific saints. Later, though, manufacturers began to produce them with specific intentions, hoping to open them to a broader market. This means along with candles with pictures of saints, you'll also find them with intentions such as *Chuparrosa* for love, *Abre Camino* for opening the road, along with other intentions such as prosperity, cleansing, luck, and so on and so forth. There's a novena for just about anything if you're willing to dig a little. But what is the difference between using an intention candle and a saint candle?

Mostly the difference hinges on one major factor: are you going to do it yourself or ask someone else to do it for you? Saints are extremely powerful and may intercede quite effectively in our lives, bringing in many blessings and much-needed change. However, if you aren't familiar with the particular saint in charge of your issue, you may not feel like you can approach them and ask for favors. That's where the intention candles come in. You may work directly with God or *La Virgen* or any of your personal angels through intention candles without having to approach a particular saint. For example, say you need a Block Buster spell to help you get through an obstacle. You could call upon St. Barbara, patron saint of demolitions, using a novena dedicated to her and asking her to remove the obstacle. Or you could just go straight for the Block Buster candle and cast the spell yourself without asking for her assistance. This might be the most appealing option for some, especially if you aren't familiar with St. Barbara. Conversely, maybe you aren't familiar with how to do a Block Buster spell or have a lot riding on the issue and don't feel confident that you can handle things on your own. In that case you can ask St. Barbara to take the reins. Sometimes it's better to hire a pro, instead of attempting to go it alone. Either way, even if I'm not calling upon a specific saint to do the work, I will always ask for the assistance of *La Virgen* or my ancestors.

Also, saint novenas are not specifically limited to spellwork. You may burn them to honor certain saints while you pray to them and get to know them. You could also burn saint candles as a thank-you gesture when they've come through for you. Ultimately, whether to use saint or intention candles is up to you and the status of your relationship with the saints. If you are using an intention candle and having no luck, I do suggest trying a saint candle with proper offerings, as they are usually stronger than we are alone and may be able to achieve what you cannot. You can also mix and match and offer an intention candle to a saint if you don't have one of their novenas. For instance if I needed extra cash and wanted to ask St. Jude, I could offer him a Call Money candle that has been dressed with herbs and oils.

The other type of novena you'll usually find is plain blank candles. These are useful for certain spells when you just need a candle of a particular color. You may also turn to these when you can't find a specific saint or intention. For instance, I have trouble finding St. Martha candles where I live, so I just buy plain green novenas and decorate them in her honor with paint or Sharpies. You may also make your own intention candles or prayer candles this way. I also like to use a plain white novena and write psalms or prayers on the glass using a silver Sharpie. Feel free to get creative.

A Brief Overview
of Colors and Intentions

We're going to briefly explore the different colors of plain novenas to choose for your specific purpose. I'd also like to go over a few of the more common intention candles you may find and their uses. Most of them are really straightforward like a Jinx Remover, but others are in Spanish or have symbolic meanings that may not be obvious to most folks.

Colors

Red: Protection, power, passion, love, marriage, speed, the Blood of Christ, family blood, male virility, strength

Pink: Friendship, love, romance, relationship healing

Orange: New beginnings, road opening, courage

Yellow: Communication, success, legal aid, the Holy Spirit

Green: Money, prosperity, heart healing, masculinity, the earth, growth

Blue: Healing, protection, tranquility, invisibility, angels

Purple: Domination, success, victory, power, loyalty, psychic power, spirituality

Black: Absorption/destruction of negativity, banishing, protection, hexing

White: Shielding from negativity, healing, holy power, purification, all-purpose

Grey: Knowledge/ancient wisdom, strength, power of stone

Brown: Court case work

Intention Candles

Chuparrosa (**Hummingbird**): Brings in a new, pure love. It's also applied to help heal a current relationship or a broken heart. The way a hummingbird sips from a flower without disturbing it is a metaphor for how it helps remove negativity without messing up the relationship.

Ven a Mi (**Come to Me**): Brings someone to you. These candles are used romantically in order to get the attention of your crush or to create situations in which you might "bump into" them out in public. This is good for bringing around a lover that you haven't heard from in a while or taking a casual flirtation to the next level. These work best on folks you already have a spark with but are too shy to make a bigger connection.

Abre Camino (**Open Road**): Clears our path of obstacles. This is used to open the doors of opportunity and is often employed when trying to reach a specific goal.

Rompe Bloque (**Block Buster**): Gets you out of a rut or a stuck situation that you can't seem to free yourself from. This is a more powerful/aggressive version of the *Abre Camino*.

Justo Juez (**Just Judge**): Used to ensure a fair ruling during a court proceeding. It can also be applied to ensure a judge condemns a criminal for his actions and justice is served (use the black ones for this). Conversely, it can be used to get an innocent person out of jail (use the white version). Just Judge candles can also be employed to get a fair ruling in any situation or to bring someone to justice even for nonlegal matters.

For example, if someone is lying about you, you can use a *Justo Juez* candle to make sure that they have to pay justly for their actions. Be careful though; justice *will* be served, and these may backfire if you are also guilty.

Tapa Boca (**Shut Up**): Stops gossip or lies.

Contra Brujería (**Against Witchcraft**): Protects against witchcraft and bad energies intentionally sent your way. Sometimes you will find these called "against salting."

Contra La Ley (**Law Stay Away**): Keeps away authority figures such as cops, immigration, bosses, and landlords.

Gallina Negra (**Black Hen**): Removes hexes and spiritual parasites.

Ajo Macho (**Strong Garlic**): Chases away evil and restores luck and health.

Del Retiro (**Retirement**): Puts an end to something, whether it's banishing bad people from your life or ending a relationship.

Rompe Conjuros (**Spell Breaker**): Breaks evil spells cast upon you.

Doble Acción Reversible (**Double Action Reversal; sometimes just** *Reversible*): These novenas are often black and one other color. They remove and send back hexes while also restoring what was taken. These usually come in three colors: red/black for love, green/black for money, and white/black for general purposes.

Separar (**Break Up**): Splits up relationships. It's usually used for ending romance but can also break up groups of conspirators.

Fixing or Dressing Your Novena

All novena candles really need is to be lit with prayer, however this practice is often taken a step further. The act of incorporating oils, herbs, curios, and energy into your novena is called *fixing* or *dressing* the candle. By doing this we are essentially programming our wants and needs into the wax so that when the candle burns it sends out our intention and our request. This process can seem complicated at first, but once you get the hang of it, it's quick and easy.

Step One: Prepping Your Novena

The first step in fixing your novena is cleansing it. Remember wax is great at picking up and storing energy. Between the factory and your altar your candles may have come into contact with all kinds of energies you don't want in your spellwork. It's best to begin with a clean slate so that we don't have any magical interference. This also empties the candle so that there is more room for our prayers and energy. For most purposes, I cleanse novenas with a mix of Florida Water and holy water in a spray bottle. I spray down the glass and wipe it in a downward fashion using a white cloth until it's dry. As I do this, I visualize each swipe of the cloth emptying it of all previous energies. You may go about this your preferred way though, such as running it through cleansing smoke or sprinkling it with salt.

At this point I stop and say a prayer while making the sign of the cross over the candle. I call upon higher powers like *La Virgen* or particular saints and speak what I want the results of the candle to be. This just helps to set the intention and build the power inside the candle.

Step Two: Make Some Holes

Once your novena is cleansed, you're going to want to poke some holes through the wax. For this I like to use a small screwdriver. An awl or an ice pick would also be ideal. Some folks like to use knitting needles or barbecue skewers. However, novena wax can be quite hard and these are likely to bend. If nothing else is around, I've been known to use a fork to just stab the wax and create some openings. There's nothing magical about this act; mostly we are just opening some tunnels in the candle so the oils can travel down further into the wax instead of just sitting on the surface. You may use a particular number of holes if you are into numerology, or just do two or three as you see fit. The holes don't have to go all the way to the bottom either. Keep it simple, and don't overthink it.

Step Three: Blessing and Anointing

Now that you've poked holes in the top, you're going to add your oil. You may choose to use a specific oil—such as a love oil for a love candle—or just a general holy or anointing oil. You can also find special oils dedicated to certain saints. Some saint oils may be purchased from their shrines around the world, and some have even been in contact with holy relics, which is pretty neat. Either way, pour a small amount into the top of the candle, avoiding the wick and aiming for the holes you've made. Once I've added my oil, I pick up the candle and rotate it side to side to get the oil to spread out nicely. You want just enough to coat the top of the candle, not so much that there's standing oil. If you've overfilled, don't worry: you can just pour some out.

Once you have just enough oil in your candle, do another blessing. To do this, I make the sign of the cross over it and say a prayer calling upon the Holy Trinity and stating my desire. For instance, if I were doing a love novena, I would say, "In the name of the Father, the Son, and the Holy Spirit, I bless and activate this candle to bring true love to me. May they be strong and kind and love me for who I am. In Jesus's name, amen." Don't feel like it has to rhyme or be a long declaration. Simple and direct are always best in this work. While I say this prayer, I hold my hands over the candle and visualize it glowing with holy light. I finish by making the sign of the cross over it to seal the intention, and then I move on.

Step Four: Herbs and Curios

The next step is to pick a few herbs—no more than five if possible—that match your intention and add them one at a time to your candle. Remember your novena is not very big so add just a little pinch of each. Every time you add an herb, bless it the way you did the candle above, by making the sign of the cross and saying a short prayer stating what you want that individual herb to bring to the spell.

Sprinkle them into the top of the candle, lightly coating the surface with the herbs. Be sure not to add too much: you should still be able to see the wax underneath. I also like to make sure none of the herbs are crowding the base of the wick, which usually leads to a small fire, lots of black smoke, and sputtering. This may affect your glass reading later (see below). At this point if you have anything else you'd like to add such as stones or curios (shredded money, saints' medals, etc.), put them in now. Before doing so, bless each item in the same manner as the others.

Step Five: Bringing It to Life

The final step in fixing your candle is to charge it up. Take the whole thing and bless it one more time, making the sign of the cross over it, and begin saying a prayer stating exactly what you need. I do this with my hands over it, while I visualize it radiating holy light. Once I have this image in place, I continue to pray and envision that the candle is filling up with my prayers and growing brighter with each word. These prayers bring it to life. I finish by sealing the work with the sign of the cross.

Some people don't do this next step, but I like to feed my candles to increase their power. In order to do this, I recommend feeding them prayers by holding the novena in both hands and praying the *Padre Nuestro* or the *Dios te Salve* three times, visualizing the power of the candle growing stronger. Other folks feed them incense by holding the candle in the smoke until they feel like it's full. This method is good too because the incense doubles as an offering to Guadalupe or any other spirits you are offering your candles to. Use whichever method feels right to you. Once you get the sense your candle is well fed, lift it high and say, "Guadalupe, Queen of Heaven and Earth, I offer up this candle to you as a sign of my faith and gratitude." Then light it up with perfect faith and perfect confidence. If you are offering it to a saint, feel free to light it in their name instead. Once a day come back and feed it more prayers and have faith that your needs will be met.

A Note on Proper Filling

I wanted to insert a quick note here because I feel it's quite necessary. The goal is to *not* overfill your novena with herbs and oils and other flammables. You may think more is better, but we never want to force our results, especially if it could put us in danger. It's become a vanity issue in the mystic community to show off your strong candle flame. Unfortunately, this has prompted a great many folks to pack their novenas to the brim with flammables and then set it ablaze like a bonfire to advertise how powerful their spellwork is. The same is happening with exploding candles. Folks have been overpacking them and then bragging all over about how powerful their magic must be because their novenas keep exploding. None of this makes you powerful; it only makes you a pyromaniac—which isn't the goal of this craft. Remember, it's a candle, not a pipe bomb. If your magic is powerful, it will have a tall, strong, steady flame that isn't the result of too much dressing material. Also trim your wick to about a half inch; having a three-inch wick set ablaze is also a hazard.

Burning Your Novena

There are several ways to burn your novenas. None of them are wrong or less powerful; it just depends on the situation. I use all of these depending on what I'm trying to accomplish and find them all to work quite well.

You may leave them burning continuously until they go out themselves. This is the most traditional way to use them, and I like to do that if it's something I'm really trying to get done quickly or with intensity. If you are going to go this route, though, make sure you do it safely, and have a plan to keep things safe when you have to leave the house. For instance I set burning novenas in my sink, which is very deep and nonflammable, when I leave. On other occasions I've put them in the large stockpot I use for canning to keep them safe. Work with whatever you have on hand.

Another way to go about burning novenas is to burn them a little each day over a number of days. This is nice because you can sometimes make them last the full seven or nine days depending on how long you leave them lit each day. You can even premeasure sections that you'd like to burn per day in order to make it last a set number of days. This always brings up the question of whether to blow out the candle or to smother it. I've heard some really dramatic reasons why you should not blow out candles. Some say you'll offend spirits; some say you'll blow the magic out; etc., etc. However, I've rarely found these to be true. If you have no other option, feel free to blow them out—just do so reverently. I personally prefer to smother them as it's a bit gentler and more controlled. One thing I will recommend, though, is if you are lighting them and putting them out after a short time, wait for the entire surface of the wax to liquefy before you extinguish the flame. This will keep the wax flat and prevent it from building up awkwardly on one side and leading to trouble burning down the line. Never be afraid to "turn off" your candles when you leave and relight them when you return.

When it comes to saint novenas, I burn those only when I'm attempting to evoke their spirit. For instance, if I am going to be saying prayers to St. Joseph, I'll light one of his candles, say my prayers, let it burn for a bit, and then put it out when I'm done. If I'm asking them for an intercession, though, I often burn one of their candles to completion as an offering and a sign of faith and devotion.

I'll also use intention candles for support for regular spellwork. Say I'm doing a protection spell or making protection charms; I'll light a protection novena at my altar while I do the work and then I'll smother and put the candle away when I'm done. Next time I do a protection spell, I'll pull it out again and relight it to add its protective energies while I work.

There's really no wrong way to do it as long as you're being safe. No matter how you choose to work with your novena candles, make sure you are always practicing fire safety. Make sure to either smother them or move them to a safe place when you leave or go to bed. Also, you may wish to purchase either larger glass cylinders or metal buckets to hold them in in case they decide to explode or get wild. Remember this is magic: the results can be unpredictable. Have a plan—and a plan B—in the event of a fire.

Seeing the Signs during the Burn

Before we get into the divination aspect of novena burning, I want to take a second to remind you that all spells, Catholic or otherwise, require faith and confidence. Too often, people use the act of divination as a way to look for all the "bad news" at best or signs that God is angry with them at worst. I want you to remove that idea from your mind before you go any further. There are no bad signs in a novena; there are only information and feedback. Your candle isn't trying to scare you; it's simply letting you know what's happening. You must also factor into your assessment of these signs what the candle was for. Each sign may mean something different based on the intention behind the candle, and we'll discuss that a little more as we go.

Tall, Strong Flame vs. Short, Weak Flame

A tall, strong flame is usually a good sign, as long as it's not a result of overfilling your candle. This means the work is flowing nicely, there's plenty of energy to burn, and the magic is sturdy. Usually a strong flame will burn the candle much faster than a small flame. This indicates that the results will come quickly but won't last. A small flame, on the other hand, shows a slow, steady delivery of the work over time. This can be useful for long-term work and is not always a sign that your spell is weak.

If the flame is small and gutters or threatens to go out, however, you may need to repeat the spell or add more power to the existing one through prayer or lighting separate candles alongside the original one.

Occasionally a candle will start out with a small flame and then later grow into a much larger flame. This is an indication that the candle might have been initially overwhelmed with the job. I see this a lot when I'm burning cleansing candles for people who have had a lot of issues happening. The candle is momentarily stunned by the enormity of the task, and then after a couple hours it takes control of the situation and the flame grows stronger. You may help it by feeding it prayers.

Conversely, if a candle starts out really strong but over time the flame weakens, I generally take this as a sign that it's mostly accomplished its job and the task no longer requires large amounts of energy. Candles that burn this way may bring heavy results quickly and then smaller results slowly over time.

Knotted Wick

If the wick forms into a ball, a knot, or a mushroom this usually represents an obstacle or blockage. I find these a lot in road-opening or block buster work. It can take some time for the flame to eat through the clump, but it's a representation of the candle's magic chipping away at your real-life obstacle. Over time, the flame will break it down and begin burning smoothly. Pay attention to where it happens in the burn and how many times it happens. Many knots indicate many obstacles to overcome. Knots that happen early in the burn signify obstacles close at hand. Knots that happen later in the burn indicate obstacles farther down the road. In most cases this is not a sign that your path is blocked; it's simply your candle informing you that it has found an issue and is addressing it. Again, this is not a bad sign, just feedback.

Noisy Wick

If the flame whistles, hisses, or crackles, it's trying to communicate with you. If a saint or spirit candle is noisy, it can indicate they wish to give you a message or they are pleading your case on your behalf. If you are trying to bind a bad spirit with your candle, the hissing and popping show it's angry and fighting back but don't necessarily mean it is overpowering the spell. Keep your faith!

Moving Flame

Dancing or flickering candles are highly energetic! These candles are putting in work, shifting and changing the landscape of our future, and can often bring about unexpected or creative results—especially if the flame is strong. If my saint or spirit candles are dancing, I take that as a sign of their presence. If the flame is small and flickers or gutters, this is a sign that either the work is not strong enough or an outside force—such as an unfriendly spirit or another worker—is suppressing it.

Spent Wick

Sometimes while your candle burns, the wick won't disintegrate and flake away. It will simply create a long, sometimes curling grey strand that no longer burns but stays attached to the wick as the candle continues to burn. I usually take these as a sign that something is being held on to that needs to be let go. For instance, if I'm working a love candle for someone and this happens, it's a sign they haven't loosened their grip on baggage or feelings from a past relationship, and that needs to be addressed.

Candles That Won't Light or Go Out

Candles that won't ignite or repeatedly go out can be stressful! But don't worry, there are many reasons for this. First, make sure there isn't anything wrong with the wick or the candle. Did you accidentally soak your wick in oil while dressing it? Or did it get wet? If you can't find a mundane reason for what's wrong with the candle, then it may be a supernatural issue. If this is a request candle for something like love or domination, the spirits may be sending you a clear no, meaning you need to think about what you are asking for and if it's the best idea. Sometimes spirit tells us no because we're either being childish or they have something better planned for us. If it's a saint candle, that saint may be refusing to work with you. Not all saints and people match up, and that's okay. You haven't incurred the wrath of anyone; they may be simply opting out.

If a candle spell for cleansing, protection, or exorcism of negative forces won't light or keeps going out, it may be overpowered. Some ill-intentioned spirit or energy doesn't want you to get rid of it, so it keeps extinguishing your candle. If you suspect this is the case, you should first place a rosary around the candle to protect it from malefic forces and then try to burn it again. I would also begin a thorough cleansing and blessing of yourself and your home while the candle burns. This can help a lot if your novena is struggling under the weight of the request.

Glass Cracks or Explodes

A broken or exploding candle can also mean a great many things depending on your situation. For instance, a protection candle cracking or busting may mean that something has overpowered it. A hex-breaking candle cracking may indicate you've broken the spell. Cracks and breaks may also signify breakthroughs. Check in with how you feel when it happens. Does it feel positive or negative? This may also be a time for divination to check what is going on. More often than not, though, breaking or exploding candles are a result of overfilling and that should be the first thing you look at when this happens. Manufacturer error is also a common issue, so always be careful when burning these.

Reading the Glass

After your candle has finished burning, you may look for information left behind by the flame and wax. This technique can be rather handy and will often give you insight into next steps.

As before, we want to take these signs simply as information and stay strong in our faith. Resist the temptation to look for "bad" signs—there are no bad signs—or signs your spell didn't work. The other thing you must remember to include in your interpretation is the intention of the candle—which will change the meaning of any sign from spell to spell. Also, be sure to take into account any mundane or manufacturing issues, which may cause a false sign to appear.

As a baseline, a "perfect" burn is a burn that is very clean, leaving the glass clear and unmarked and little to no wax in the bottom. This is essentially what you want to see, but occasionally there are anomalies you'll need to be able to interpret. Be sure to wait until the candle has finished burning and the glass has cooled before attempting to read the signs.

Black Smoke

The first thing everyone becomes concerned about is black smoke. When burning a novena, you may notice the flame is putting off puffs of black soot that begins coating the glass with a dense layer of smoke. Most folks begin to panic when they see this, but what it truly is is an indication that negativity is being removed from the situation. For instance, if I'm doing a road opener, healing, or cleansing spell, I like to see some black smoke. It lets me know my novena has burned through some negativity or removed something nasty.

If the smoke goes halfway down the glass or farther, I take that as a sign that the candle was overpowered by this negative energy. This doesn't necessarily mean that anything is after you, though. For instance if it was a road opener spell, it may be indicating that there was a huge blockage that the candle was trying to remove the whole time, and though it may have chipped away at the blockage, I wasn't able to finish opening the road with just that one candle.

Either way, when you see black smoke, it's an indication you may want to do some cleansing and then try the spell again. You may find that the next candle you light for that intention burns clear or, if you burn several in a row for the same intention, they get progressively clearer as they work through the nastiness. If there's just a little soot near the top, it's nothing to worry about.

Conversely, on the rare occasions that I do curse work, I like to see a lot of black smoke. In this situation it can be an indication of doom and negative power developing. Or if I'm doing domination work and the candle turns black, that means the target is fighting it.

Always remember to take into account what the candle is for because that can change the interpretation of the signs.

White Smoke

White smoke is the counterpart to black smoke. Sometimes you'll find that your candle is coated in a thin layer of light grey or white soot. This is a great sign! This is an indication that God, the angels, or the spirits have heard your request and have agreed to help. This is the best sign you can get during a burn.

Uneven Smoke

Uneven smoke may show up as black or white or a combination of both. By uneven, I mean it's not equally distributed across the glass and may be heavier in one area than another. This is a sign that energy is in motion and things are rearranging or on the move. That's good because that's generally the whole purpose of burning a novena: to move and redistribute energies. This is also a sign that the results may be a little up in the air or certain things need to shift before the results appear. For instance, if you are trying to get your boyfriend to move closer to you but he's in another state, some other things will have to readjust—his job, his housing situation, family, etc.—before he can move.

Clouding

Clouding is often confused with white smoke because they often look quite similar. Clouding happens when a thin layer of wax is left on the inside of the glass, causing it to look frosted. You can determine if it's white smoke or clouding by rubbing the inside of the glass with your finger. If it wipes off, it's white smoke. If it doesn't come off or if it feels waxy, it's clouding. This is a sign that you may not be seeing things clearly or may be overlooking something. For instance, if it's a candle for a job that clouds up, it may be trying to tell you that there's a golden opportunity in front of you that you aren't paying attention to.

Leftover Wax

A layer of wax left in the bottom of the candle indicates that you need to take action in the physical world in order to bring the results to fruition. This is the classic case of putting in the legwork along with the spellwork. For example, if you burn a candle to get a job, make sure to actually pass out résumés and seek employment. If you don't put in any real-world effort, it won't be effective.

Rings

A lot of times your candle will show faint rings of wax around the glass at certain intervals. These are usually read as units of time you may have to wait before your results come in. For instance, if you count three complete rings, it could indicate the results will come in three days, weeks, months, or years—depending on how big the request was. Broken rings show you a *possible* range of time and should be read with the complete rings. For instance, if you count three complete rings and two broken rings, that means you will have to wait at least three units of time and possibly up to five to see results. Using this technique I've been able to predict the arrival of results down to the day.

Novena Spells

A Hex-Removing Novena

Has someone cast a hex on you? A curse? A jinx? Given you *Ojo*? Use this simple spell to remove all kinds of malefic spell-work including *Mal de Ojo*.

You'll need:

1 black novena candle (Intention candles such as Black Hen, Spell Breaker, and Jinx Remover are also options here, as are white candles, but black is best.)
Anointing oil (Options include Uncrossing oil, Cast Off Evil oil, Hex Breaker oil.)
Agrimony
Rue
Salt

To begin, cleanse your novena candle so that it's empty of foreign energy. Once that's done, stand and hold the candle, focusing in on the curse that is on you. Try to tap into how the energy feels and bring that feeling to the surface. Starting at the top of your head and moving downward, rub the novena on yourself in deliberate intentional strokes. As you do this, pray that all the negativity be taken off you and visualize the candle sucking it up like a vacuum, trapping it inside. Continue to do this until you feel completely cleansed, making sure to pay special attention to the back of your neck, head, shoulders, heart, genitals, palms of your hands, and soles of your feet. If you come across places or energies that seem sticky or unwilling to be vacuumed up, make the sign of the cross over the area with the novena to help draw it out.

Once that's done, fix your novena candle using the oil and herbs listed above. Bless it with the intention that it destroy any negative energy or spellwork, and call upon God or *La Virgen* to aid you in your deliverance from evil. There's no need to feed this novena as you've fed it the hex that was on you, but you may still pray the *Dios te Salve* or the *Padre Nuestro* three times to charge up its hex-breaking power.

Once your novena is lit, anoint yourself with the oil in the sign of the cross (forehead, chest, left shoulder, right shoulder), as well as the palms of your hands and the soles of your feet. Pray the *Padre Nuestro* three times.

Chuparrosa Novena Spell for New Love

Chuparrosa candles call upon the spirit of the hummingbird to aid us in all matters of love. These are not generally used to cast a love spell on a specific person, but to bring a new love into your life.

You'll need:

1 Chuparrosa *novena candle*
Honey
Rose petals
Vervain (or catnip)
Nutmeg (or cinnamon)

Cleanse the candle, and dress it lightly with honey instead of oil. This helps bring sweetness to the work and also acts as a lure for the hummingbird spirit. When using honey, you want only enough to coat the top; too much will smother your flame. Sprinkle a little of each herb on top of your novena. As you do this, pray for the type of love you are looking for. Don't focus so much on personal traits, but more on the feeling you want them to bring you. When you finish, say a meaningful prayer to the hummingbird spirit asking it to guide this special love to you, then say the *Dios te Salve* over the candle three times to charge it up. This is best done and lit on a Friday.

Tip: Powdered spices like nutmeg or cinnamon will cause your novena to smoke like crazy. It's best to use cinnamon chips or whole nutmeg that you've crushed into smaller bits than the powdered version.

Chuparrosa Novena Spell for a Broken Heart

Chuparrosa candles are not just for bringing in new love; they are also incredible healers of the heart. When experiencing heartbreak, we often wish something will come along and help us mend our broken selves. This spell is to facilitate that healing.

You'll need:

1 Chuparrosa *novena candle*
Honey

Rose petals
Vervain
Angelica root pieces
Hawthorn leaves

Cleanse your novena and dress it lightly with honey to sweeten the situation and draw in the hummingbird spirit. Sprinkle the herbs on top of the candle and pray for the healing you seek, asking Guadalupe to send the hummingbird spirit to you. Then feed the candle your grief. Hold it and tell it everything that you are sad about. Cry it out while you do this, and really send your agony into the candle and ask that the hummingbird spirit carry away your sadness and heal your heart. This is best done on a Friday, during a waning moon. Repeat as necessary.

Chuparrosa Novena for Reconciliation

You didn't think we were done, did you? The third and final reason people call upon the spirit of *La Chuparrosa* is for reconciliation between lovers. Sometimes you both say things you didn't mean or let outside things get in the way of your happiness. To help bring a lover back around, use this recipe.

You'll need:

1 Chuparrosa *novena*
Holy water
Honey
Balm of Gilead buds
Rose petals
Lavender flowers
Rose incense

Cleanse the candle as usual, then bless it with a sprinkling of holy water. Dress the candle with honey to sweeten the situation and draw in the hummingbird spirit. Add the herbs while praying for reconciliation, and ask that Guadalupe send the hummingbird spirit to you for assistance. If you have a personal concern—such as hair, fingernail trimmings, etc.—you may add this to the candle, but it's not necessary. Once you're done and have added the herbs, pray the *Dios te Salve* over the candle three times. Feed it rose incense and light it on a Friday. Reconciliation work is best done soon after the breakup. Miracles happen, but if it's been a year and they are in a happy relationship, your chances are much slimmer (and it's also rude).

Abre Camino Novena Spell

Abre Camino means "open road," and this candle is used to do just that: open a road. We use this when we are trying to get to a goal but there are obstacles in the path. A road-opening spell goes down the path ahead of us and smooths the way. It's a bit like having a guy go ahead of you with a machete as you hike through the jungle. Abre Camino is also the name of a special plant that's known to open the road.

You'll need:

1 Abre Camino *novena candle*
Holy water
Anointing oil (Road Opener oil is best, or orange essential oil will work in a pinch.)
Abre camino *or* vervain *(While* Abre camino *grows only in the tropics, vervain is readily available.)*
Five-finger grass
Cinnamon
Lemon balm
1 small key (optional)
Abre Camino *incense*

To open a road, cleanse your novena and bless it with holy water. Dress it with your chosen oil as usual. Bless each herb, then sprinkle them into the novena. Say a final prayer, asking for the roads to be opened and that obstacles be removed between you and your goal. Ask and believe that Guadalupe sends an angel before you to prepare the way. As you do this, if you have an old small key, push it into the wax like you are putting it in a lock to open a door. See in your mind the door opening and the path clearing out in front of you. Feed your novena with prayer and *Abre Camino* incense. This is best done on a Sunday.

Block Buster Novena Spell

Sometimes a Road Opener is not enough. Sometimes you need less of a machete and more of a stick of dynamite. In this case, you should go with a Block Buster spell! Use with caution, however: when this opens the road, it also has a tendency to pick you up by the seat of the pants and toss you down the road as well, so be prepared for action!

You'll need:

1 Block Buster novena (or an orange, yellow, white or purple novena)
Anointing oil (You can use Block Buster oil, Road Opener oil, or orange essential oil.)
Black salt (or regular salt, or crushed black peppercorns)
Sulfur
Saltpeter
Abre camino *or vervain*

Cleanse your candle and dress it with oil as usual. In a small bowl, combine the black salt, sulfur, and saltpeter. As you do this, say prayers that the obstacle in your way be blasted apart and your road opened. It's often effective to pray to St. Barbara (patron saint of demolitions) and offer the candle to her, but you can work with God or *La Virgen* as well if that's more comfortable for you. Either way, when you are done, add this mix to your novena. It will act like spiritual gunpowder. Bless and pray over the *abre camino* or vervain, asking that it help open the roads as well, then sprinkle it on top. Feed with prayer and incense. This is best done on a Sunday.

Tapa Boca Novena Spell

Tapa Boca (Shut Up) novenas have long been used as a way to stop *chisme* (gossip) and shut the mouths of those spreading it.

You'll need:

1 Tapa Boca *novena candle*
Anointing oil *(Shut Up oil works best; if you don't have it, use a small amount of lime juice to coat the surface.)*
1 *lime*
Black peppercorns
Red pepper
Alum

Cleanse your candle and dress it with the oil before rubbing a wedge of lime around the rim of the candle. Sour things like lime and alum bind the tongue and mouth. In a mortar and pestle, grind the other ingredients while praying for the troublemaker's mouth to be shut. Pray that your name gets lost in their throat and their tongue burns every time they talk about you. Sprinkle the mix on the candle as usual and feed the candle with incense and prayer. This is best done on a Tuesday or Saturday.

Prosperity Novena Spell

Sometimes we need a little help making ends meet. That's okay— we've all been there. Here is a candle spell to help bring in that extra money. Remember a couple things when it comes to money magic: First, it's easier to make your work more lucrative than it is to make money appear out of thin air—though it does happen! Second, prosperity magic loves a good realistic number. So, take the time to calculate exactly how much money you need and for what. "I need $300 to make rent" is much more effective than "Send money."

You'll need:

1 Prosperity novena (sometimes called "Call Money" or use a plain green novena)
Anointing oil (Prosperity or Money Magnet oil are best.)
Cloves
Cinnamon
Five-finger grass
Pyrite gravel (or gold mica powder)

Cleanse and dress your candle in the usual manner. I also recommend taking a Sharpie to your novena and writing the amount you need on the glass. Bless and sprinkle the herbs into the top of the novena, along with the pyrite or mica powder. Feed this candle with prayer and incense. This is best worked on a Thursday.

Contra La Ley Novena Spell

Contra La Ley is roughly translated as "Law Stay Away" and is very important work in these times. This is work dedicated to keeping authority figures away from vulnerable communities, including making sure that immigration stays away from our loved ones who may not have papers.

You'll need:

1 Contra La Ley novena (or a white or blue plain novena)
Holy water

Anointing oil (Law Stay Away or Invisibility oil is best, but a
*   protection oil can work as well.)*
Fennel seeds
Oregano
Black mustard seeds
Black cat hair

To begin, cleanse your candle and bless it with holy water. Dress it with the anointing oil in your usual manner. Bless and add the fennel seeds and oregano; these are extra helpful plants for keeping the law away, as well as meddling individuals and narks. When you are done, take your novena and place the black mustard seeds in a ring around the very outer edge of the wax, so they are pressed against the glass. Black mustard causes confusion. You should bless them and pray over them before adding them, being sure to ask that they cause confusion in any authority that comes near, causing them to overlook any vulnerable people. Next take the black cat hair and, using scissors, snip some into the candle as well, so the hair lies on top. Black cat hair is good for invisibility. Feed this with many meaningful prayers for protection. If you are in a high-risk community, I would keep these on hand and either light one anytime the law comes around or keep one lit in the home around the clock.

Protection Novena Spell

Sometimes, we all need some protection! Whether it's from evil spirits, witchcraft, or the guy next door, it's best to have some sort of protection set up at all times.

You'll need:

1 red, white, black, or blue novena candle
Holy water

> *Anointing oil (Fiery Wall of Protection is a favorite, but any protection oil will do.)*
> *Rue*
> *Black peppercorns*
> *Devil's shoestring*

Cleanse your novena, bless it with holy water, and dress it with the oil. In a mortar and pestle, combine the rue and peppercorns while praying for protection from all harm. Sprinkle the mix into the candle along with bits of the devil's shoestring and light. Feed it with prayers for protection (the St. Michael Prayer is an excellent choice) and incense. This is best done on a Tuesday or Sunday.

5

Los Santos

Have you ever looked around at your life and wished you had help? Someone with special skills—a professional—who could give you some advice and help you through whatever it is that's going on? Lucky for you, those folks exist and they are just a prayer away. The saints are many, and they are mighty. Each has the ability to help you in their own unique way, and usually they are more than willing when asked to intercede.

Saints are a very special group of spirits that I greatly enjoy working with. They are generally safe to approach, which is sort of unusual when it comes to spirits. They don't tend to be vengeful or territorial and generally operate from a place of love and understanding. They also tend to be okay with working together, so if you feel the need to call on more than one saint for a particularly difficult situation, you may.

While they are much less volatile than their more exotic counterparts, you must respect them and show your gratitude, or else they will refuse to work with you. Some may refuse to work with you anyway: certain saints are notoriously picky about the kinds of people they will help. If you find that to be the case with a few of them, don't get discouraged or take it personally. Find those who want to work with you, and over time you'll build a small team. Don't take the lesser-known saints for granted either! Everyone wants the big ones—Michael, Peter, Anthony, Joseph, etc.—on their side, but the saint you've never heard of may have been waiting forever for you to notice them!

All saints can do just about everything. That's something you need to remember. Too often folks focus in on their specialty, and then toss them aside if that's not exactly what they are looking for. Every saint is skilled at healing, turning away evil, removing hexes and curses, and general favors. However, sometimes there is something that is just not in their wheelhouse for whatever reason. When this happens, I find they usually refer me to a colleague. Suddenly, I'll have a different saint on the brain—usually one I haven't worked with before. I'll begin to see their image in various places or hear their name often. It's like they're trying to reach out from their side and offer help. When I look, that saint is often at least loosely associated with the issue I'm having. Feel free to follow these trails and find out where they lead. You may meet a new saint, or you may receive a favor from a usually taciturn saint with the message of "Just this once." You truly never know.

Working with Saints

So the big question on everyone's mind is: how do we work with saints? Before we even begin to answer that, we have a few things to check off our "to do" list. First things first. When was the last time you cleaned your house? Like really cleaned it. This is important for spiritual—and personal—hygiene and should be done regularly anyway. Messes and clutter attract bad energy and spirits and do not create favorable conditions for saints or any other higher beings of light. When it's your first time meeting a saint or bringing their statue home, it's important to be presentable. Clean your home physically, and cleanse it energetically. (See the *Limpias* chapter for how to do this.) This creates an excellent environment for them to get to know you. Also take a shower, or at least wash your hands. If you are dirty, that may transfer to the sacred space as well. After you've worked with a saint for a while, they don't seem to care as much if your socks are on the floor or if you haven't showered, but for your first introduction, try your best.

Make sure you have a space for them cleaned, cleansed, and ready. If I have a new statue, I will also bathe the statue in a mix of holy water and Florida Water to clean and cleanse it so that it is pure. (Other things can go into this cleaning mix too depending on what you have on hand, like herbs or other special waters.) The space doesn't have to be big. It can be a small table or one section of a shelf—it really doesn't matter as long as it's stable and can safely support a few candles. It can even be a simple cloth or mat that you put out when you need and pack away when you are done. Just make sure that it works for your needs and the room you have available.

You'll also need at least one candle. It can be any kind of candle, but I prefer to work with white candles or a novena with an image of the saint. Novenas are extremely helpful because they cover multiple bases: they provide an image of the saint, a light, and they usually have prayers to the saint written on the back. If you can't find a novena, you can simply light any candle—white is preferred if you don't know the saint's associated color—and print off an image of them from the internet to place in the space. You'll also want a glass of clean, cool, fresh water set out as well.

Each one of these items has a purpose and a significance. The flame acts as a beacon, drawing in their attention and energy. It also functions as an offering to honor their spirit and provides light and warmth to them and the world. The image gives you something to concentrate on when working with them and helps you focus on their spirit and energy. When you upgrade to a statue, it's believed that a part of them begins to inhabit the statue. No matter what kind of image you are using, you'll want to speak to it like the saint is sitting right in front of you. The glass of water serves as both an offering of cool refreshment to the spirit and a conduit for their energy. Water is an excellent conductor and the most spiritual of all the elements. It helps to cool the energy of the altar space and filter out negativity. The surface of the water is a liminal space where water and air meet, so it creates a small window for saints to come through and interact with our world. For these purposes the water glass is an essential part to all interactions with spirits and saints.

Once you have the space set up, you may begin to work. Light your candle, and set out your water. Light some incense if you have it. Begin by saying a prayer to God or *La Virgen*, asking for protection and guidance from the most high. At that point you may start to say prayers to the saint.

Now, folks disagree on whether or not you may ask for favors on first contact. It really depends on the spirit you are working with. Larger spirits like deities, Orisha, etc., have much better things to do than hang out waiting for you to ask for something and can be rather offended if you begin that way. However, the main spiritual purpose of saints is to watch over and help humankind as agents of God. It's their job to intercede on our behalf when we need it. This doesn't mean they are contractually obligated, though, and some can be less than friendly if you step out of line. So mind your manners, say please and thank you, and always pay them for their work. If you choose to ask them for a favor—whether it's upon first interaction or much later after you've formed a relationship—you should always leave offerings.

Offerings to saints can be nearly anything. Certain saints have specific things they are known to like. For instance St. Expedite loves his pound cake. St. Martha likes sweet wine. St. Joseph has a thing for lima beans. But overall some good general offerings are wine, flowers, homemade food and treats, candy or chocolate, and donations made in their name to churches and charities. As you get to know them, you'll begin to figure out what things the saints you are working with like and what things they aren't fond of. Feel free to try new things; I often find I'm surprised by what they are drawn to.

Your offerings can also carry a message or help influence the energy you are trying to bring forth. For instance, offering coffee tends to wake spirits up and get them moving. It helps them work faster toward your goal and adds energy to a situation. If you are asking for favors involving love, giving them flowers—especially roses—will reinforce that energy. So feel free to play around with this concept and see how they respond.

Beyond offerings, when working with spirit altars, you must remember that these are portals and must be maintained. Open portals in the home can become dangerous if not properly cared for or utilized. I was taught to think of it in terms of hot and cold energies. Hot energies bring in negative entities, and cool energies bring in positive energies and entities of light. If your altar space gets too hot, it can attract less than friendly spirits, some of which can masquerade as helpful spirits such as saints and ancestors.

Things that bring in hot energy are things like dirt, dust, mess, urine, feces, sexual fluids, moldy or stale offerings, dead flowers, hot-colored decorations, etc. Remember these have a cumulative effect. Just because you have something red on your altar doesn't mean it's a big demon magnet. But if that is paired with several other factors—like dead flies in the spirit water glass, and your cat taking a pee on your altar cloth—then it may become a problem. This is why it's important to keep your working spaces tidy and to always bathe or wash your hands before doing your work.

Things that bring in cool energies are things like cool-colored decorations, fresh flowers and water offerings, Florida Water, and a general clean and tidy atmosphere. Refreshing the glass of water on your work area frequently with cool, clean water is a great way to cool the altar energetically, as are fresh white or cool-tone flowers. Wiping your altar space down with a rag soaked in a mix of water with a splash of Florida Water in it is a great way to clean up and cool down the surface as well.

Before engaging in this work I always begin by tidying the space both physically and energetically. You don't want any nasty entities hanging around when you open a portal and yourself to their influence. I always either burn some herbs that banish evil or spray some Florida Water around to clear the space. This makes way for the good spirits you want to work with.

When doing this work, if the spirit you are working with—saint, ancestor, or otherwise—seems strange, gives you a nega-tive feeling, or asks for something concerning—like borrowing your body temporarily or to harm another—say no and banish it in the name of Jesus Christ (holy water is great for this). Then cleanse everything down again. Certain unholy spirits can mimic others and they tend to be a bad deal. It is a good practice to get a sense for whatever spirit you are working with before you invite it in further and begin to work with it. Always check your gut. If it's not right, don't go forward. If your house is properly warded though, and you cleanse routinely, it's generally safe to move ahead. This is also why it's important to keep your prayers specific: "Dear (specific saint)" or "I'm praying directly to Grandma Gigi," etc. If you just begin talking to the air asking for help, just about anything can take that as an invitation to interact with you.

Now that you have a basic understanding of how to begin working with the saints, we will get into a few of the ones you may want to connect with. This book was written with the intention of being something unique and useful to the modern Mexican American person and a way of preserving some of our culture. So I wanted to do something special in this chapter: I will be introducing you first to some important figures in Mexican American history who have become known as Mexican folk saints. Most cultures have folk saints—people who were part of the community and were famous for something in particular. These were often heroes in some way who continued to help their people even after death, though the Church does not acknowledge them as canonized saints. I like working with Mexican folk saints because it feels a bit like asking a *tío* or *tía* for help when you need it. As fellow Mexicans, they understand us, our culture, and our values. It's said that when traditional Catholic saints won't help you, folk saints will.

Mexican Folk Saints

In this section we will be covering a small handful of the folk saints worked with across Mexico and the United States. Please note that this is not all of them, and in fact, this barely scratches the surface. If you are curious or like the idea of working with Mexican folk saints, I encourage you to look into them more deeply! They are a very fascinating group, and many of them are still performing miracles to this day.

Juan Soldado

Juan Castillo Morales is the man that we affectionately call Juan Soldado, which literally translates to "Soldier John." He was born in Jalisco, shortly after the turn of the 20th century, and grew up to be a soldier working in Tijuana. You see, that time in history was particularly bad for Tijuana. It had been a popular place for American tourists—still is—who would go there to have a good time during Prohibition. Then in the span of two short years, Prohibition ended in the United States and Mexico declared gambling illegal. This meant thousands of people lost their jobs all over, but Tijuana was hit particularly hard. This led to civil unrest and an increased military presence to help maintain control. Enter Juan Castillo Morales, soldier and early twenty-something guy just trying to get by.

On February 13, 1938, eight-year-old Olga Camacho Martínez disappeared. The police searched for her all day but were unable to find her. According to legend, her brutally murdered body was found near the military housing area. When Juan Castillo Morales was ordered to retrieve the body by his superior officer, someone saw him and assumed he was the murderer. Some say his superior officer was the one who had killed the girl and framed Juan on purpose, but truly we will never know. Folks thinking he was the murderer quickly formed into a mob. People were already angry just given the state of the city at that time, and this murder was the match that lit the entire powder keg.

The crowd grew and rioted outside the police station and city hall for two days, eventually setting fire to both, then preventing firefighters from stepping in to help. The military ended up intervening and shooting or arresting many of the rioters, but even then could barely get the city under control.

They decided the only way out was to use Juan as a scapegoat. They pushed through a quick trial, found him guilty, and sentenced him to death by firing squad. However, even that seemed to take too long, and while transporting him, military officials encouraged him to run—which he did. As he fled, he was shot dead, saving them the time and energy it would have taken to put together a formal firing squad. As the heat of the hysteria died down, people began to realize that he had been wrongly accused and began to see their error in judgment and misdirected anger. Many folks began to pile rocks where he had died, but the military quickly took them away and washed away the bloodstains.

That's when the miracles began.

According to legend, the blood returned to the pavement the next day. The military kept trying to clean it away, but it kept coming back. Word spread, and folks began to visit both this site—where a small shrine now stands—and his grave in the cemetery. It was said that his tomb would bleed and you could hear his voice proclaiming his innocence. Some folks even tell stories of his ghost walking through the cemetery. Soon folks from all over were coming to these sites. Many believe that if a person is killed for a crime they did not commit, they are given a special place in heaven close to God. This means he would have a better chance of getting word of your struggles to the Almighty than most.

Like many folk saints he is petitioned for hopeless situations. He also is called on to watch over members of the military, those crossing the border into the United States (some say he was running toward the border when he died), vulnerable children, and those falsely accused or incarcerated for crimes they did not commit. However, like most saints he can also be called upon for all manners of healing, love, financial issues, and overcoming addiction. His feast day is on June 24, and I associate him with the colors green, yellow, pink, and white.

Jesús Malverde, the "Angel of the Poor"

The story of Jesús Malverde is widely known in Mexico as he is one of the most popular folk saints. He is hailed as a Robin Hood type who would steal from the rich in order to give back to the poor. Not much is known about him for certain, but it's believed that his story is an amalgamation of several real tales of bandits from the area. Whether he existed as reported in the legends or not, we may never know. However, many people swear by his presence and ability to give aid when petitioned. He cares deeply for the poor and is not judgmental about dealings outside of the law. Due to the latter, he is a popular saint among drug traffickers and one of several spirits known as "narco saints."

Jesús Malverde was thought to have been born and lived in Sinaloa. It's believed his name was actually Jesús Juarez Mazo. He was later called "Malverde"—roughly translated as "Evil Green" —as a nickname. He grew up watching the socioeconomic hardships of his people and was said to have witnessed his parents' death. The story changes around whether they died of a treatable disease or starvation, but the central point of truth is that poverty inevitably killed them. After their passing, he began his life of crime: stealing from the rich and bringing the money and goods back to provide for his people in Sinaloa.

After a long and infamous crime spree, he had proven himself a worthy adversary and had yet to be caught. So a government official challenged Malverde, saying that if he were able to steal something valuable—the object changes from a sword in the governor's house all the way to the governor's actual daughter—he would be granted a pardon for his life of crime and allowed to go free. According to the story, Malverde pulled off the heist and was able to steal the prize without getting caught. This infuriated the government officials and brought the full force of their vengeance upon him. It's uncertain how he died. Some say he was caught and hung by police. Others say a friend betrayed and killed him. Either way, that was allegedly his last crime and attempt at redemption. In most stories he wasn't given a proper burial, and his body was left to rot out in public to make an example of him.

To this day people petition him for all sorts of things including money for the poor and help out of poverty or hopeless/trapped situations. Many miracles of healing and protection from the law are attributed to him, and he continues to be a popular folk saint known all across Mexico and parts of the United States. I associate Malverde with the colors white, black, green, and gold. He is celebrated on May 3, which is the alleged anniversary of his death.

Teresa Urrea, "Saint of Cabora"

Santa Teresa is a folk saint known especially well to the Yaqui and Mayo peoples. It was said that she fell seriously ill at the young age of sixteen in the year 1889. During this illness she began to experience religious visions and believed that she had been given divine healing powers by the Blessed Virgin. After she was well again, she began to heal the sick. Soon news of her abilities spread far and wide, and more than a thousand people came and camped near her to seek her aid. It was said that she had no fear of the sick and would touch open wounds and contagious folks with bare hands. She would even sleep among them and was always said to be friendly no matter the illness or circumstances.

Her political downfall happened after she became a symbol of justice and the fight for equality. She was well-known for giving sermons and pointing out injustices both within the Church and outside of it. Her name became a popular battle cry for resistance fighters as *La Santa de Cabora*. Though there is no evidence that she was actually involved in the resistance herself, she was exiled from Mexico and is still known as a political insurgent. I associate the colors white, light blue, green, and pink with her.

El Niño Fidencio

José de Jesús Fidencio Constantino Síntora, better known as El Niño Fidencio, was a famous Mexican *curandero* born in 1898. It was said that he never developed sexually, causing him to remain childlike with a soft voice and devoid of facial hair. He was one of the most influential healers in Mexican history and was known for his somewhat unique cures, some of which required making offerings to a local pepper tree and bathing in a mud puddle. Strange as they may be, the cures worked extremely well! On other occasions he performed miraculous surgical operations without anesthesia and without causing pain to his patients. To this day you can find *curanderos* who claim to channel his spirit in order to perform healings for their clients.

Catholic Saints

St. Martha (Santa Marta)

St. Martha is my most beloved saint! She is best known for sassing Jesus in the Bible. You see Jesus and his followers made their way to a place called Bethany where they stayed at an inn. Martha ran the inn and was quite busy cooking, cleaning, making beds, and keeping the home together. She is patron saint of all service workers including—but not limited to—innkeepers and waitstaff. Martha's sister, Mary of Bethany, was completely enraptured with everything Jesus had to say and would sit at his feet all day and listen to him. This enraged Martha, who needed help around the inn. She was clearly not one to put up with the patriarchy, even back then. Due to this many modern Christians look down on Martha and tut about how she should have been more like her sister. Still, they can't deny that Martha not only became a friend of Jesus and one of his followers, she was also an important character in the Bible and was one of the seven myrrh-bearing women that found Jesus's tomb empty. There is also some debate about whether or not Mary of Bethany and Mary Magdalene were the same person. If this is true, that would make Martha the sister of both Mary Magdalene and Lazarus, essentially making her Jesus's sister-in-law.

There are many stories that accompany biblical figures and what they went on to do after Jesus was crucified. It was said that Martha and her sister continued in the mystical teachings of Jesus and spent their days in prayer and meditation, while traveling and continuing his work. There is one lesser-known story in which Martha comes across a town under siege by pirates and causes a river to rise and sweep away all the marauders. Another story is the most famous about her and the reason why she is normally depicted with a great dragon. You see, Martha is part of a very special group, female dragon slayers. Throughout history, men have often been hailed as the ones dealing with dragons, but women have had their fair share of standoffs with the scaly beasts themselves. Martha is my favorite monster wrangler because, unlike her male counterparts, she took it alive.

Many people connect dragons to St. Margaret, but she didn't really face a dragon—it was the devil in disguise. She also didn't defeat it herself; she gave it indigestion, which is not the same. Martha, however, bravely faced off against a dragon herself. The story goes that in her travels she stumbled upon a village terrorized by a great dragon that was making off with their children and livestock. Hearing their plight, Martha agreed to help. Some stories say that she engaged the dragon in the city. Others tell that she went down to a cave by the river where the dragon lived and met it there. It is said that she hit it with holy water, making it unable to breathe fire, then when she showed it the cross, it was unable to move. She then charmed it by singing hymns and eventually was able to tie it up with her girdle strings—resourceful, and a powerful symbol of early feminism. With the dragon subdued she took it with her into the city to show the residents that it was all okay now and the dragon would not harm them anymore. The people, overcome with fear, mobbed and killed the dragon.

This sad tale is allegedly the seminal story for "Beauty and the Beast." Some folks believe this because it deals with the idea of a young maiden charming a terrible monster into being good, but people murder it out of fear and their inability to understand. While I'm not sure if this is true, it's clear that Martha was extremely brave and tenacious!

In some circles she's known as "Martha the Dominator," which has less to do with her Catholic persona and more with her other spiritual synchronicities with African and/or Caribbean spirits disguised as saints. However, I have found that even in her Catholic form she's willing to help in this manner, especially when it comes to dominating men. As the patron saint of service workers she's especially adept at taming unruly or problematic bosses in the workplace and often called upon for this work in particular. Some folks have the idea that she won't work with men, but I have worked with her for some time now and find her to be quite pleasant—though snarky on occasion—and willing to deal with me. In fact, she was the first saint I ever worked with.

A St. Martha Spell to Sweeten Your Boss

Anyone who has ever worked in the service industry can tell you what a jerk most bosses can be. They are often looking for things to get on your case about, and when they aren't, they're looking for reasons not to pay you more. This is a spell designed to get your boss off your back and to appreciate you more.

You'll need:

1 green candle (or a novena to St. Martha)
1 jar
Raw sugar
Boss Fix oil
A sample of your boss's handwriting (or business card)
Lavender
Gravel root
Calamus root
Oregano (optional)
1 jumbo purple candle

On a Tuesday, light the green candle as an offering to St. Martha and say a prayer asking for her assistance. Tell her exactly what's going on with your boss and what you want to change. Fill your jar most of the way up with raw sugar, and add a few drops of the Boss Fix oil. I find raw sugar to be a little more reliable and steady than white sugar, but work with what you have. Take the handwriting sample and anoint it with the Boss Fix oil and say a prayer over it asking that they appreciate you and leave you alone! Bury this paper in the sugar. Add the lavender to the jar, and pray that it help calm them so they feel more relaxed around you. Stir it in. Add the gravel root, and pray that they give you a raise for all of your hard work. Stir it in. Add the calamus root, and pray that they are made willing to do what you ask. Stir it in. If they tend to be a helicopter boss that's always looking over your shoulder, add the oregano, and pray that they stay away from you while you are working. Stir it in. If at any point the handwriting comes up to the surface, just push it back in toward the bottom of the jar. Pray over the jar once more and seal it shut. Anoint the large purple candle with the Boss Fix oil and affix it to the top of the jar.

Every day for seven or nine days, burn a little bit of the candle—you can premeasure it if you like—until it's all gone. Pray to St. Martha every time you light it. By the time it's done there should be a noticeable improvement in your boss. Keep the jar, though, and if they begin to act up again, get another purple candle and repeat the candle-burning part of the process.

St. Lucy (Santa Lucia)

St. Lucy is a beautiful spirit. Her name Lucy or Lucia means "light" or "lucid," and she's often called upon to bring clarity, insight, illumination, and the brilliant white light of God. I find her to be very protective but gentle as she simply radiates her light. Due to her connection with illumination, she's called upon not only to bring protection from the darkness, but also to introduce clarity to situations, reveal the truth, blind enemies so that they may not spy on us, and enhance our natural psychic abilities. (This last is also partly due to her connection with eyes, which we'll get to in a moment.)

St. Lucy's story of martyrdom is similar to many others. She was a young maiden in Syracuse who had pledged her life to God in a time when Christians were being persecuted for their beliefs. She was said to be very beautiful, and a young Pagan man had asked to marry her. But she wished to remain pure and virginal in her service to the Lord. Her mother was very sick, and Lucy had been going to the tomb of St. Agatha often to ask for her help. One day St. Agatha appeared to her and told her that her mother would be healed only through an act of faith. So Lucy convinced her mother to give away Lucy's dowry money to the poor and turn away the Pagan suitor—which she did—and she was healed of her sickness. The enraged suitor turned her in to the authorities. The governor ordered that Lucy be defiled in a brothel, but when they came to take her, they found her to be immovable. Many men tried to haul her away but could not. Eventually they hitched her up to an entire team of oxen, but even their brute strength could not budge her. So, changing tactics, they piled up wood around her to burn her, but the stack would not light. Eventually, one of them stabbed her though the neck with a sword, which brought her death.

At some point during all of this she lost her eyes. The details on that are the foggiest. Some say that it was part of her ordered punishment and the soldiers took them out. Others say that her suitor greatly admired her beautiful eyes and she clawed them out herself to try and get him to leave her alone. Either way, when her body was exhumed later on, her eyes had been restored. That's why St. Lucy is often depicted holding a plate with eyeballs on it, as well as a palm frond—a sign of martyrdom as well as victory over evil.

A St. Lucy Spell to Cleanse a Home

This working is excellent for removing the stagnant or negative energy that naturally accumulates in a home. I find this to be the spiritual equivalent of giving your home a good vacuuming. It doesn't necessarily fix everything, but it really freshens the place up. Don't forget to always clean your home physically before cleansing it spiritually.

You'll need:

1 white candle
1 egg
Salt (blessed)
1 drinking glass
Water (Holy water or regular water is fine.)
1 St. Lucy prayer card

To remove negativity and bring peace and illumination to a home, begin by carving a cross into the white candle and blessing it in the name of the Holy Trinity. Light the candle and set it aside. Say a prayer to St. Lucy over the egg, and continue praying as you wipe yourself downward with the egg to purify yourself (see the chapter on *limpias* for detailed instructions). Your energy affects your home, so starting with yourself can help create the shift you need. Once done with that, dispose of the egg in an outside garbage. Next, add three heaping spoonfuls of salt to the glass and fill it the rest of the way to the top with the water. Ask St. Lucy to bring peace and light into your home as you stir the water to dissolve as much of the salt as you can (it may not all dissolve and that's okay). When you're done, place the glass on top of the prayer card in a prominent place, along with the candle. Let it sit for nine days and notice any changes that happen to the water. At the end of the nine days, dispose of the contents—I prefer to flush them down the toilet—and clean out the glass with white vinegar. Don't drink out of the glass; instead use it to repeat this process as needed.

A St. Lucy Spell to Reveal the Truth

If you are meeting with a person or a group and wish for the truth to be revealed to all, you can ask St. Lucy to illuminate it for you.

You'll need:

1 white candle
1 shallow bowl
Holy water
Salt (blessed)
1 St. Lucy prayer card

To bring about the truth, begin by carving the sign of the cross on one side of the candle along with the words "the light reveals the truth." Say a prayer to St. Lucy over the candle and ask that she reveal the truth. Affix the candle to the bottom of the bowl and set it aside. Pour the holy water into another container and add a small pinch of salt—this is to cleanse away the lies. Stir it counter-clockwise nine times while asking St. Lucy to chase away the lies with her light and leave only clarity and truth. Gently pour the water into the bowl with the candle and light it. Place the bowl with the prayer card under it either on the table where you will be having your discussion or nearby—preferably up high—and the truth will be revealed. Pay close attention because people may not spill their guts—though I have seen this happen—but may trip up and let something slip, which you should be ready to catch.

St. Margaret/Marina of Antioch (Santa Margarita)

St. Margaret, also known as St. Marina, is a fascinating saint. She is known as one of the "Fourteen Holy Helpers" and was one of the voices that spoke to St. Joan of Arc. Her story, like many of the others, is that of a Christian woman living in a time when the religion was persecuted. Some say she was the daughter of a Pagan priest but converted to Christianity. This is only in some versions, though. Like many female saints, she too had a male admirer who was Pagan, and when she turned him away, she was outed as a Christian and given over to the authorities. She was tortured and then thrown into a dungeon where she had to face off against the devil. It was said he took many forms to antagonize her, including that of a dragon, which swallowed her whole. However, she wore a cross, which irritated his stomach, and he was forced to throw her back up. Gross, right? Well, it gets better. The next day she was supposed to be executed, first by burning and then by drowning, but neither worked. It is said the people watching this were converted by witnessing these miracles. Finally, like many others, she was killed by beheading.

Though her story is fairly standard, there is a depiction of her that has always stood out in my mind. Not much is known about the image, or where it came from, but it has circulated widely. What is depicted is St. Margaret beating a demon with a hammer. If that is not a mood, I don't know what is. This image has stuck with me for quite some time, and I often think of it in times when I am faced with negative entities. You see, folk magic has a long history of putting power in the hands of the people, and if a demon shows up, we are taught not to fear but to take care of business any way we need to. This may or may not include taking a hammer to the devil.

St. Margaret Exorcism Spell

To draw off negativity and negative entities from a home and banish them, use this spell.

You'll need:

1 black novena candle
1 condition oil (Destroy Evil oil, banishing oil, or something similar can be used. In a pinch use eucalyptus, rosemary, or camphor essential oil instead.)
Salt (blessed)

To begin, cleanse and bless the novena candle, praying over it and asking that it remove, bind, and banish all evil in the home. Take the candle around the home and run it around all doorways, windowsills, baseboards, and any thresholds present in the home. As you do this, pray and visualize the novena picking up all the negativity and evil like a magnet and trapping it inside. Once done, place the candle on its side on a table and roll it away from you three times. Dress the candle with the oil you chose, and lay a thin but sturdy layer of salt across the surface of the candle. Salt is a great purifier and destroyer of evil, so we are purifying and destroying the negative energy trapped in the candle. Once that's done, light the candle and say prayers every day it burns to St. Margaret to bind and banish all evil and demons from your home.

St. Christopher (San Cristóbal)

St. Christopher's is a tale known across the world. He was said to be a fearsome giant of a man with a wild face and towering over others at nearly eight feet tall. He wanted to serve the greatest and most powerful king, so he went and found one with that reputation and served him until he found out that the king feared the devil. So he went in search of the devil instead, thinking he would be the most powerful. After learning that the devil feared Christ, he converted to Christianity. As a means of service, he began to help people cross a wide and raging river that was deep and dangerous. Many people had died attempting a crossing, and he saw this as an opportunity to use his enormous size and formidable strength to help others.

One day an infant child appeared on the shore and asked to be taken across, so he did. Halfway over, it was said that the child suddenly became extremely heavy upon his shoulders, as if Christopher were carrying the weight of the whole world. They both nearly drowned, but Christopher made it to the other side. There the child revealed himself as Christ and explained that Christopher had indeed withstood the weight of God. The child then vanished. Christopher went on to be martyred when he was beheaded for converting Pagans to Christianity.

Many people call upon St. Christopher to protect them while traveling. Based on his story, I have found some other reasons to call upon him, which he seems happy to help with. First, he is a great saint for road-opening work, as he is helpful for carrying you over and through obstacles. The other issue I have found he's quite handy at fixing is immigration problems. For many people, immigrating legally to the United States is quite a bit like trying to cross that wide and raging river. I've called upon St. Christopher to help folks with these issues on several occasions, and each time it's met with great success.

St. Christopher Immigration Spell

This work is intended for those who are facing a court date or any other legal situation where their ability to enter or remain in the United States comes into question. This is most effective when used for people with pure intention and limited criminal activity.

You'll need:

1 Just Judge novena candle
1 white or orange candle (If it's a family situation, use one
    chime candle for each member of the family.)
Road Opener oil
Vervain
1 St. Christopher prayer card

To begin, cleanse all the candles. On each stick/chime candle you are using, carve the sign of the cross into the wax on one side, and the words "(person's name), Welcome to America" on the other. Making the sign of the cross over each candle, bless it in the name of the Holy Trinity, and announce "(person's name), Welcome to America!" Coat each candle with oil and roll it in the dried vervain. Bless the Just Judge candle by holding it, praying the *Padre Nuestro*, and asking that justice prevail and they be let into the United States. Set the novena on your working surface. When you're ready, light it and lean the prayer card to St. Christopher against the base of the novena, so it stands upright facing you. Place the candles for each person either in a candleholder or affixed together on a small plate. Light them, and pray the *Padre*

Nuestro, followed by prayers to St. Christopher asking that they be carried through the legal process of immigration successfully.

St. Michael the Archangel (San Miguel)

St. Michael is unique because he was not a living person like the others. He has always been an archangel and a favorite religious figure among the faithful. He is a powerful and highly energetic protector to call upon for help in any dangerous situation. His most famous triumph is the day he led an army and cast Lucifer out of heaven. This is why he's often depicted slaying a demon with his legendary flaming sword. St. Michael is known as the "keeper of all works" and therefore can make or unmake any spell ever cast. He can also exorcise any demon and protect against any foe. He is a saint that likes to be on his own shelf/altar—not because he's territorial (though he is rather proud) but rather his energy is very powerful and can inadvertently push other spirits out. Many people expect him to be very snobby—as a lot of angels are—but I've found him to be a bit like a religious Dean Winchester type. He's very cool and will do whiskey shots with you if you ask. His colors are red, blue, and white, and garlic is sacred to him.

A St. Michael Spell for Protection
This is a spell commonly known as "Fiery Wall of Protection," and I call upon St. Michael every time I cast it.
  You'll need:

1 white candle
4 red candles
Fiery Wall of Protection oil
Rue
Garlic

Cayenne
1 *white plate*

Start by cleansing all the candles. Then carve your name—or the name of whoever needs protecting—into the white candle and a cross into each of the red candles. Dress each candle with the oil and roll it in a mix of the herbs. Affix the white candle to the center of the white plate—which represents you—and each of the red candles so that they make a cross pattern around the white one. They symbolize protection in the north, south, east, and west. Once that is done, light the candles while saying the St. Michael Prayer (page 26). If you wish, you can encircle the plate with the rest of the herb mix clockwise for extra protection.

St. Jude (San Judas Tadeo)

St. Jude has a very special following in Mexican American households around the country. However, his veneration was not always smooth. Early on it was said that folks didn't want to pray to him for fear of accidentally evoking the presence of Judas who betrayed Christ. This meant that when folks did eventually begin praying to him, he was so eager that he granted powerful miracles, which led to him being known as the patron saint of lost causes. Interpreted rather loosely in Mexican culture, this title has even come to represent people who would be considered "lost causes" by society—criminals, drug dealers, mafia members, and more. His following is actually made up of the same people who work with *Santa Muerte* and other folk saints like Jesus Malverde. Furthermore, due to a handful of illegally copied portraits of him that inadvertently changed his staff from his right hand to his left, many folks believe that St. Jude will also answer prayers for mischief and cursing of enemies.

He is the saint I suggest most people work with instead of *La*

Muerte, as he can do the same things, and always comes through, but is much less wrathful. Since his usefulness extends across the board and he doesn't have a singular specialty, it's hard to give a specific spell for St. Jude. However, I will say this, if you are opening a new business, I suggest putting his statue on a small table behind the door. It can be placed next to or on top of a dish of coins. Burn green candles and incense to him while praying for customers to come and thieves to stay away. You'll be amazed at what happens.

Santo Toribio (St. Toribio Romo)

The last saint that I would like to discuss is Santo Toribio, our esteemed patron of illegal border crossings. Though St. Christopher is also very helpful to those who are attempting a trek across the border, Santo Toribio is the most notable helper of those making the journey. In this situation I would call on Toribio first and foremost and, if necessary, also call on St. Christopher. There are many, many stories of Santo Toribio appearing in the desert to give aid to those who are lost or dying on their way to the United States. Even Mexican people who are not attempting a border crossing but end up stranded for some reason or another near the border have reported that a man matching his description has appeared and helped them out of their crisis.

I myself had a life-changing encounter with him. Though a small instance, it changed how I viewed the saints and spirits that watch over us forever. You see, it was right after the border crisis began and it was brought to light that thousands of people were being held in cages at the border. I was enraged and saddened by this news, and I got the idea to petition Santo Toribio for help. So I laid out my offerings with a glass of water, lit a novena to him, and said some prayers. I did not feel his presence at first, which is normal, so I left everything on my altar and went about my business.

A couple hours later I heard a sound like a bell that alerted me to his arrival. Going into my altar room, I found him standing there, looking disheveled and distraught. The first thing I noticed was his overwhelming thirst. He is a saint who spends his time in the desert helping people dying of thirst, after all. I immediately went and fetched him an even larger glass of water and even opened a La Croix and placed them on the altar with the other offerings. He explained to me that he was well aware of the border situation and he had been there for weeks already with Jesus and Guadalupe, doing their best to comfort and bring peace where they could. You see, humans have been given the gift of free will, which cannot be messed with. This means that if humans choose to put other humans in cages, then they as saints can't interfere. I had never seen a saint look as tired as he did right then. Usually they are very well put together and beaming with energy. I never thought that our actions here on earth could affect them so deeply—but they do.

Sometimes our saints and spirits need our help. So in times of crisis, please give offerings and prayers to your saints and spirits so that they may continue to assist us the best they can.

Simple Santo Toribio Spell for a Border Crossing

When I know someone is about to attempt a border crossing, I do this novena to help them travel safely.

You'll need:

1 piece of paper and a pen
1 Santo Toribio novena
Holy water

On the piece of paper write the name of the person who is

attempting the crossing. If you have a picture of them, that's even better, but work with what you have. Using the holy water, make the sign of the cross on the paper and pray for safety and guidance for that person. Cleanse and bless the candle, praying to Santo Toribio that he watch over them. Place the novena on top of the paper and keep it lit until they are safely on the other side. If you need to, use a second or third novena to keep the flame going until you receive word they are safe.

La Muerte

Santa Muerte is the most infamous of all the Mexican spirits. Sure, people fear *La Llorona*, the weeping ghost who stalks children, but she floats out on the fringes where she's easily avoided. *Santa Muerte* is everywhere. She's in the home, she's in the streets, she's in the palm of your enemy's hand—and she will come for each of us in the end. People fear her and adore her in nearly equal measure. Though they are completely separate spirits, some say she is the shadow of *La Virgen de Guadalupe* or her dark counterpart since she's the "anti-mother": the one who removes us from this earth and births us into the afterlife.

Her name literally translates to "Holy Death" and she is just that: the spirit, or saint, of death. This is what sets her apart from other popular spirits and something that we need to remember: She is death itself. She is the taking. Many deities, such as Hades, Hel, Hekate, are all gods that rule over the *place* you go when you die and therefore are often placed in the same basket. However, *Santa Muerte* is the *action* of death. She is your own death as much as she is death as an idea. Folks see her as a *representative* of death and take that at surface value without really considering all that means for this spirit. More on that later.

No one is truly sure where *Santa Muerte* came from. Some say she, like Guadalupe, survived colonization under this new disguise and is actually an Aztec goddess known as Mictecacihuatl. This would be fitting as Guadalupe and *Santa Muerte* go together like the two sides of a coin, with *La Virgen* birthing us into this world and *La Muerte* removing us from this life. However, others say she is actually a European spirit brought over by the Spanish known as *La Parka* who is also a skeletal Grim Reaper–type depiction of death. It's hard to say what her true origins are; she seemed to just appear out of nowhere one day in Mexico City. Doña Enriqueta Romero is often credited with erecting the first public *Santa Muerte* shrine in a neighborhood in Mexico City known as Tepito, an area infamous for its heavy crime, drug cartels, and rising body count. This seems fitting because *Santa Muerte* is often seen as a "narco saint" or a patron saint of drug dealers as well as thieves, criminals, and murderers. Some shun any representation of *Santa Muerte* as anything other than a loving mother, but her spirit is complicated, as is her following.

In this section I will strive to give a clear and honest look at the spirit known as *La Muerte*. My opinions on this subject may be considered unpopular, but they certainly aren't unfounded. I know that some of you may be offended by what I have to say; however, I would rather upset some folks than lead people into danger.

The Open Arms of Santisima

One thing that has helped make the following of *Santa Muerte* one of the fastest-growing cults in the world right now is her open-door policy to all people. Death will come for everyone regardless of their history, lifestyle, or social standing. She loves everyone in equal measure. Death is also devoid of a moral compass. She doesn't strike down just the bad people or the good people; she is separate from good and evil. Death simply is. Her place isn't to judge you for your choices or your life. That's God's job. Her job is to simply take you, no matter who you are or what you've done. This means that even those who have done terrible things are accepted by her, no questions asked. This quality instantly made her patron saint of criminals, sinners, murderers, sex workers, drug dealers, and other people who live their life against the rules of the Church. She is also patroness of the marginalized: people of color, the poor, the handicapped, members of the Queer community, and other nonconformists that society and the Church have rejected. This was so important for Mexicans at the time of her appearance because many of them had already been forced to resort to a life of crime and sin as a means to feed their families. Having a holy spirit around to care for them—even one that can be terrifying and destructive—was exactly what they needed.

This open-door policy is also a point of serious tension between her followers. Since magic, witchcraft, and spirituality have become mainstream in the United States, folks have made the mistake of assuming that the spiritual practices from cultures of color are fair game and have sought out whatever traditions they feel like joining and distributing among themselves. This includes *Santa Muerte*, and now that she's gaining popularity, many people are flocking to her who don't necessarily need her. People who were outcast from society, and had little choice in who they fled to for comfort, have now found themselves having to share space under the wings of *Santa Muerte* with people of privilege. These are often the same people who had marginalized them to begin with, and that's just one more hard pill for oppressed and indigenous communities to have to swallow. Please keep this in mind if you are from outside of the community or are otherwise privileged with plenty of options both in spirit and in life. Is it necessary for you to work with *Santa Muerte*? Is the help you are seeking available to you in the form of any of the hundreds of saints and spirits willing to hear your call instead? Are you marginalized to the point that no one but death itself will accept you? These are things to consider before you decide to engage in this work.

Furthermore, as more folks from outside the community flood her fan base, they also begin to erase her cultural roots by rejecting her Catholic style of worship (don't do this) and producing new lore and stories that were never part of her canon. As colonized people, we take the erasure of culture very seriously. That's one of the reasons why when folks come to me—most often from outside the community—and ask how to start working with her, I often ask them why they chose *Santa Muerte* specifically. An overwhelming amount of the time they just shrug and say, "I'm drawn to her." In recent years being "drawn" to something has developed into a sort of free pass for accessing indigenous culture and leapfrogging over important traditions folks just don't want to observe. I am drawn to Jason Momoa, but that does not mean he wants me in his house. Also remember that *Santa Muerte* can be dangerous (more on that in a moment). So, unless a person has a serious reason for needing to, it's best to work with the infinite number of other spirits available to them. This helps not only limit the potential danger associated with *La Muerte*, but also protect our culture.

A Word of Caution

We're about to get into the finer points of working with *La Muerte*. However, before we go any further, we need to have a talk. I know that *Santa Muerte* is really, *really* cool, and you've heard how she works quickly and grants every wish without fail. Of course, you want to sign up for that! Who wouldn't? But we need to be real for a moment and have a very serious discussion about what it could mean for you and your family if you begin to work with her. Remember, the Mexican people began working with her because many of them were out of options and had no alternative. You, on the other hand, most likely do. I urge you to think long and hard before you decide to evoke *Santa Muerte* and explore other spirits and saints that are not the actual act of death before turning to her. I know in a poetic, philosophical way, death is beautiful. It really is. But death in real life is ugly and can destroy everything you've ever held dear. When you begin working with *Santa Muerte*, you are literally inviting death into your home to roam amid you and your family. This is not a joke, a metaphor, or a game. You must respect this spirit and this work.

We must first remember that death is without moral compass or loyalty. This does not make death or *Santa Muerte* evil; it does, however, make her fickle. *Santa Muerte* is known for her willingness to cut down our enemies—sometimes literally—if we only should ask. People really get excited about that part and feel powerful working with her, thinking that nothing can touch them. However, if she has no problem cutting down your enemies whether they deserve it or not, do you think she'll think twice about doing it to you too? Remember, death knows no loyalty. When competing devotees of *Santa Muerte* go head-to-head in magical battles, it generally comes down to who's giving the better offerings. It's never personal—it's business.

The other thing we need to be aware of is that she does require payment. Every time we pray to a supernatural spirit, we are writing a check for a job we need done. At some point, that check gets cashed, and if you aren't prepared to pay up, then you might be in trouble. If you don't pay sweet St. Lucy, she may simply refuse to help you in the future. If you don't pay *Santa Muerte,* you're in for a rough ride. Working with her is like hiring the mob. They get the job done, usually quickly. Still, it's easy to find yourself as their next target if you are unable to pay. I know several people who have had their lives ruined because they promised her something they couldn't afford or didn't actually intend to give to her and she took her revenge. It's not unheard of for folks to begin working with her and within a year lose everything—houses, money, loved ones, etc.—and some even end up committing suicide. I've also known several people who were not specific about her payment and came home to find their pets or farm animals dead. She'll take what she wants, when she wants it. Are you prepared?

At the end of the day, working with *Santa Muerte* is largely unnecessary for the average American. Most of the things you would want to ask *Santa Muerte* for can be easily be granted by any number of saints and spirits that don't pose a risk to both you and your family. Try any and all angels, saints, and holy spirits—remember Guadalupe?—first. Only in the event that none of them help you—and you really have no other choice— should you turn to *La Muerte*. If you are wanting to hang out with "dark" saints or be part of a "bad kids" club, hang out with San Judas Tadeo or Jesús Malverde. Even Santa Marta is considered a dark saint by some, due to her willingness to dominate others.

Getting Acquainted with Death

The thing you should know right from the start is that *La Muerte* does not work with everyone. While we are all equal in her eyes, she may or may not choose to grant you favors or otherwise build a relationship with you. If your novenas won't light, your flames are weak, or she doesn't come through for you, you may have to face the fact that she isn't accepting your invitation. This is her prerogative, and it needs to be respected. I get a lot of messages from folks in this predicament, and instead of just accepting it, they try to force the relationship. You have to remember that it's not about you, so don't take it personally.

If she does respond to you, though, it is important that you get to know her. This is not done only through ritual, but also through getting to know how the Mexican people venerate her and following their traditions. There are many spirits of death from around the world, but *Santa Muerte* decided to show up in Mexico for a reason. This means it is important to go with her traditional veneration, and this means embracing Catholicism. There is a huge tendency for folks to get a hold of her image and try to blend it with Neopaganism or otherwise strip away the Catholic overtones. Many claim her origins to be pre-Christian, but the truth is that we do not know that for certain. *Santa Muerte* came out of Catholic Mexico and needs to be honored in that way, because she chose it herself. If you are uncomfortable with this, please remember that it's not about you, it's about her.

When you begin working with her, you will quickly realize she has quirks. She does not like to share her altar with other spirits, especially Pagan idols or foreign deities. She will allow Mexican folk saints, Guadalupe, and some Catholic saints like St. Jude to be on her altar, but her statue must be the largest. I've heard it's best to work with her in tandem with St. Michael and Guadalupe to balance the energies, and I don't think that's a bad idea. Do not combine her with spirits from other traditions like the Orisha or Hekate, and definitely don't put her in the same space as other wrathful spirits such as Kali Ma. Furthermore, some folks will tell you to engage in "saint punishing" in order to get her to give you what you want. For instance, they'll tell you that if you take the scythe from her statue and tell her you won't give it back until she fulfills your request, she'll work harder for you. Don't do this—really. If you take from her, she is likely to take from you, and I can guarantee that you won't like it.

Unlike the other saints, *La Muerte* has a job outside of helping us on earth, which means when you approach her, you need to form a relationship with her before you ask for favors. Light novenas to her, say prayers, give gifts, and learn to pray her specific form of the rosary. Show her that you care. After a few months, you may begin making requests. Please understand, though, that working with *Santa Muerte* is a relationship, not just hiring someone for a job on occasion. This is a lifelong commitment. Are you ready for that?

The Colors of Death

There are several models for distinguishing the different faces of *La Muerte*, most commonly the three-color model and the seven-color model, both of which refer to the color of the robe she is depicted wearing. Classically she's known to be worked with in white, red, and black; however, modern forms add the four other colors of green, blue, gold, and purple. Both models are valid and equally used throughout the world. I prefer the three-color model because it really covers all the bases you'll need.

The seven-color model is more expansive and allows for more specificity, but truly, it doesn't matter. It's all the same spirit at the end of the day, regardless of which color you are working with. Below we will cover the three major forms of *Santa Muerte* and their different personalities and specialties.

La Blanca

La Blanca is the white-robed form of *Santa Muerte*. This is the aspect of her that you should get to know first. *La Blanca* is the most docile of her forms and deals with purity, healing, protection, forgiveness, and illumination. She is excellent for cleansing and exorcism work and forms an impenetrable shield of light around her devotees. Her light can expose the truth, illuminate your path, or elevate your spirit. Since she is associated with purity, she may also be seen as a road-opening spirit, purifying the path ahead so that we may walk free of any obstruction. She can be called upon to purify the body of illness or the home of evil spirits. She also deals with the forgiveness of sins and purifying the soul. Her scythe cuts away our ties to unhealthy relationships and the shackles that once held us back. White is the color of bone, and therefore, she may open the door to the ancestors and help with mediumship. Her light may help illuminate our other psychic abilities as well.

La Blanca prefers pure offerings. This includes dishes of salt and sprinkles of holy water or Florida Water. She likes white flowers, white wines, silver tequila, eggs, green apples, and herbs such as rosemary, lavender, mint, and sage. White candles may be burned in her honor.

La Roja

La Roja is the red aspect of *Santa Muerte*. Red is the color of flesh and blood. She deals with all things carnal, including war, combat, lust, passion, sex, and love. She is the impassioned, rosy face of *La Muerte*. She is called upon to go to war with our enemies, especially in circumstances concerning love and relationships. She's known for returning stray lovers and burying—sometimes literally—the other woman or man who tried to take your lover from you. She's known to be temperamental and quick to bite back should she suspect you are getting cheap or aren't paying her enough attention.

La Roja likes romantic offerings of jewelry, money, liquor, and perfume. She also has a particular fondness for chocolate and red candies, red roses, red candles, and red wine.

La Negra

If you skipped directly to this section, go back to *La Blanca*, and start there. *La Negra* is the one that everyone wants to work with. She's the black-robed form of *Santa Muerte,* who is infamous for her destructive powers, her deft hand with necromancy, and her ability to both throw and protect against all manner of hexes—not to mention her willingness to slice up your enemies. (Just remember anything you ask for comes at an equitable price.) Most folks think that sounds really great—who doesn't want a supernatural bodyguard? They don't stop to consider that she will also be in their home and around their family. Remember, death knows no loyalty. *La Negra* is the most dangerous of all her aspects and should be approached with great respect and care. Be very clear with what you are offering to pay her and make sure you will be able to deliver. Not paying her may be the worst mistake you'll ever make.

La Negra likes black candles, black licorice, dark chocolate, cigarettes, and cold hard cash.

7

Limpias

Curanderismo is an age-old folk healing tradition found through-out almost all of Latin America. Each place has its own traditions and methods, spanning from Mexico City to Puerto Rico and beyond. Curanderismo is one of the main rivers that feeds infor-mation, traditions, and techniques into American Brujeria. Both are heavily influenced by Catholicism and rely on God, the saints, and *La Virgen* for healing and blessing. In many places in Central America, doctors are hard to find or even nonexistent. This means that folks have no one else to fall back on except *curanderos*. These folk healers often treat a wide range of both physical and spiritual sicknesses from an upset stomach to broken bones, curses, fevers, and the occasional possession. These healings are often miraculous in nature and frequently defy western medicine with simple techniques such as massage, herbal remedies, and prayer. *Curanderos* and brujos are often considered two sides of the same coin: it's all technically magic but *curanderos* deal with cleansing and healing, and brujos are traditionally seen as destroyers. At the end of the day, though, magic is magic.

In this chapter we will cover the art of the *limpia,* otherwise known as spiritual cleansing. This is done in several ways, and you will find the methods that you are most comfortable with. These techniques are essential to have on hand. You never know when you may stumble onto the spiritual battlefield and be the victim of *Mal de Ojo,* a ghost, a curse, or something else entirely! If you or a loved one finds themselves in this predicament, it's important to know how to fix it—and quickly. Let's begin.

Who Should Call Themselves a Curandero? Who Should Give Limpias?

Literally anyone can benefit from and use these techniques as necessary. By reading this chapter you will be well equipped to face off against the most common spiritual issues that you might be confronted by. However, does this make you a *curandero?* No. Should you go out and start charging for *limpias?* Also no.

The title *curandero/a* is not something one simply adopts or earns by taking a course (even if you received a certificate). It's customary to spend years learning firsthand from a bona fide *curandero* before even considering the title. I even know a couple people who are very educated and skilled in the art of Curanderismo and have studied under elders for years, but do not call themselves *curandero/a* because the title has not been given to them *by the community*. You see, it's customary to not take on the name until your community sees you as such (same with brujo/a). This takes time and work. If, after learning from a real *curandero/a,* your community begins to call you a *curandero/a*, you may adopt the title proudly. If you don't have proper training and bestow the title of *curandero/a* upon yourself, you can end up in deep trouble both spiritually and legally. People rely on *curanderos* for real medical assistance, and if you don't know what you are doing, you can really hurt someone or even be liable for someone's death.

However, we all find ourselves in a spiritual pickle every once in a while, and this means that knowing these techniques can really come in handy for helping yourself and your family when needed. Here in the United States, real *curanderos* are few and far between, so we often have to handle this business on our own. Most of us who grew up in the culture have been given a *limpia* by a family member or know someone in the community who does this work unofficially. While you are learning, I suggest using these on yourself first so you get to know the process and what it feels like before attempting to help anyone else.

Herbs and Plants

Before we get into the specific techniques, it's important to have a general knowledge of some of the plants associated with this work. Here are some of the common types that can be used and their attributes.

Albahaca

Albahaca or basil, particularly "holy" basil or tulsi, is frequently used for *barridas* and often considered all-purpose or general use. Basil is strong, fragrant, protective, and adept at chasing away evil, which makes it an excellent candidate. It's also easy to grow and widely available.

Romero

Romero or rosemary is often employed as a sweep for people who need physical healing, as well as for people who are suffering from depression or anxiety. It's known to help cheer people up, bring clarity to the mind, and improve memory.

Ruda

Ruda or rue is an extremely powerful plant that is used only on special occasions. It's all-purpose but has a particular affinity for helping when someone is facing spiritual warfare. This includes removing and protecting against malefic witchcraft, *Mal de Ojo*, and evil spirits. It can be applied in baths, smoke cleansing, and sweeps. Don't forget that rue can cause skin irritation and should not be used around pregnant women or women who are trying to become pregnant.

Espanta Muerto

Espanta muerto, which is often loosely translated as "ghost chaser," is another very powerful plant that should be used only when absolutely necessary. This plant is extremely adept at removing ghosts or spirits that might be tormenting the individual. It's also very useful for breaking hexes and curses sent against them. You may use this plant in smoke cleansing, baths, or as a sweep.

Preparing for the Limpia

Before we embark on the actual process of cleansing, there is some literal housekeeping that needs to be done beforehand. Attempting to cleanse someone in a cluttered or unclean environment is never a good idea; it's like trying to give a pig a bath in the middle of a mud pit. The same goes for trying to cleanse someone when you yourself are energetically dirty. You'll simply be sluffing off your bad energy onto them as quickly as you are cleaning it. Not to worry though, there are many ways to remedy this problem. Let's talk preparing the space first . . .

Cleaning the Home

When cleaning the home of clutter, mess, and stale energy, it's helpful to follow a few rules for maximum results. The first thing to learn is the direction of cleaning. When cleansing, sweeping, and mopping, it's always best to go top to bottom and back to front. For instance, if your house has two stories, start on the second story and work your way down to the first floor. Then on the first floor always work from back door to front door. Or if things are really bad and you are washing the walls too, start at the top of the walls and wash downward, then mop the floor back to front. This helps collect everything and make sure it's swept or pushed out. Remember, we always determine this from the home's true front door as well. For instance, if you have a front door, but your family always comes into the home from the side door, you still want to orient yourself using the home's front door, not the door you use most frequently. If you're still not sure which door this is, judge based on which door your house address numbers are closest to.

The other thing you need to make sure to do is open all the doors and windows. This is very important. Not only does it help you air out your home, but it lets the bad energy you are trying to get rid of escape easily. If you are doing a smoke cleansing, I always recommend opening all closets, cupboards, and wardrobes as well—even drawers if you have time. Evil spirits and bad energy like to hide in these places. Be sure to get under beds as well.

When cleaning the home, you may put together both the acts of physically cleaning and energetically cleansing into the same action. For instance, sweeping or vacuuming and mopping can both clean your dirty floors and chase away bad energy. If you are sweeping or you have carpet and have to vacuum, you may make a dry mix of salt and cleansing herbs, such as rue, agrimony, basil, rosemary, lavender, etc., and sprinkle it across your floor to sit a moment before sweeping it away. Be sure to sweep top to bottom and/or back door to front door for maximum results. Sweeping straight out the front door is also best, but most of us use a dustpan, which is fine too as long as every other procedure is followed. If we sweep front to back, it's considered an act of bringing energies into the home.

Floor washes are a whole new subject, though, and can be quite complex! These extremely useful mop bucket concoctions can really pack a wallop when it comes to spiritual cleansing. A floor wash can strip a home of bad luck, remove a curse, exorcise evil spirits, and more. Apart from removal, floor washes may be used to draw in protection, love, luck, money, and more (we'll touch on that later). Mopping follows the same directional rules, such as top to bottom, then back to front. Most floor washes are herbal concoctions that are added to your regular mop water with your usual detergent or preferred cleaner.

Basic Floor Wash

This is a recipe I use frequently for general cleansing and maintaining good energy in the home. It can also be diluted 1:1 or more with water and used in a spray bottle for countertops and bathrooms. It's a great cleaner and helps strip away the bad energy.

You'll need:

1 large jug distilled white vinegar
3 sprigs fresh rosemary
1 large lemon
1 lime

Open the large jug of distilled vinegar and drop in the sprigs of rosemary. Peel the lemon and cut the peel into strips and drop them in as well. Juice the lemon and the lime and add the juice to the jug as well—you may have to pour a little out to make room in the jug before you begin. Once it's all added, shake it up while praying the *Padre Nuestro*, and let it sit overnight. The next day it's ready to use. I add a few splashes of this to a bucket full of hot water and Fabuloso and us it on my floors. Don't use the wash undiluted because the vinegar can be too acidic for some surfaces. I also add a splash of this to cleansing baths to strip away bad luck, but we'll talk about those later.

Floor Wash to Remove a Curse

If you feel your home is cursed, it can be rather frightening! But don't worry, you can cure most nasty curses with a proper floor wash.

You'll need:

1 spoonful agrimony
1 spoonful rue
1 spoonful salt (blessed)

Begin by praying over each herb, asking them to help remove the curse upon your home. Bring a medium saucepan of water to a boil, and add in the herbs. Cover, and let simmer over low heat for ten to twenty minutes. While that's going, fill your mop bucket up halfway with tepid water and add in the salt. Stir in your favorite detergent, and while you are doing this, pray the *Padre Nuestro*. Remove the saucepan from the heat and carefully strain the liquid into the mop bucket. Mix well with your mop and get to work!

Floor Wash to Remove the Dead

Is your home haunted? Do you feel like one of your family members accidentally brought home an unexpected visitor with them that you would like gone? Use this floor wash to remove evil spirits from the home.

You'll need:

> 2 *spoonfuls dried* espanta muerto *herb or a handful of the*
> *fresh stuff*
> 1 *spoonful salt (blessed)*
> Creolina *(a type of tar water sometimes called La Bomba)*

Bring a medium saucepan full of water to a boil. Pray over the plant matter and ask that it expel all ghosts and evil spirits from your home. Add the plant matter to the pan and cover. Reduce heat to low and let it simmer for ten to twenty minutes. Meanwhile, fill a mop bucket halfway with tepid water and stir in the salt and a capful of Creolina. Pray over the water. Once the plant matter is done brewing, strain the liquid into the mop bucket and stir with the mop. Be sure to clean in every corner, and under all furniture. Spirits will hide and evade exorcism at all costs.

Generally, I begin this process by announcing that it is their time to leave. I feel that it is only fair to give proper warning before evicting them. Beware using this, though, if you have friendly house spirits you would like to keep around, as they will be affected as well. This is to be used only on special occasions. Be careful when handling Creolina—it's very powerful and will burn your skin on contact.

Apart from floor washes, you may also cleanse your home with smoke or incense. The herb most commonly used is sage, but you may also burn rosemary, juniper, cedar, white pine, copal, and frankincense to cleanse a space. If you feel your home has been the target of *brujería*, burning a combination of rue and agrimony is useful. I recommend cycling through so you are not leaning too heavily on any one plant ally. This helps ensure that there is enough to go around in the future. I like to follow up a floor wash with burning herbs for cleansing, just to get anything that may still be hanging around.

A Lime *Limpia* for *la Casa*

Citrus fruits have long been used to clean up bad energy. Limes are the most cutting and work best for the tough jobs. Lemons are also deeply cleansing and have the bonus of being lucky. Oranges are the least cleansing and are most often used in road opening and love work. To cleanse the energy in your home and absorb any evil or *mal brujería*, you'll need just a few items.

You'll need:

1 white candle
Limes (use either 3, 7, or 9 limes)
A knife
Salt
A white plate
Cloves

Light the candle and gather your limes, saying prayers over them. Using the knife, cut them down the middle lengthwise and once down the center in the form of a cross. Don't cut all the way through though, just most of the way. You should be able to pull the limes open exposing their inner flesh without them falling apart. Once you've gotten them all open, begin to pour salt onto the plate. Don't be shy: you're gonna want a layer about a quarter-inch deep. Place each of the limes in the salt and sort of squash them around in it so they nestle in. Take three cloves and push the sharp ends into the inner meat of each of the limes. Then salt them, pouring it down into the middle of the fruit.

Again, feel free to use it liberally. Set the plate full of limes in a prominent place in the home for three, seven, or nine days, and they will soak up all the bad energy in your home.

Pay attention to how the limes react over the next few days. It's normal for them to turn yellow around the edges or even a little brown if you leave them for the full nine days. However, if they turn dark brown or black, begin to mold or smell bad, or otherwise start to rot, it's a sign that they've absorbed something quite nasty. If it's really severe or happens quickly, you may need to do a deeper cleansing on your home.

Cleansing Yourself

In the same way it's important to cleanse your home before doing a *limpia*, it's important to cleanse yourself of both dirt and negativity. If possible, take a shower and/or a spiritually cleansing bath before doing any healing or cleansing work. At the very least, wash your hands, and give yourself a *limpia con huevo* (see page 141), which doesn't take much time and will make a world of difference.

Once that is done, I always put a few drops of Florida Water into my palm and then rub my hands together. As I do this, I begin to pray. I pray to God for protection, power, and cleansing. I pray to Jesus and *La Virgen* and ask them to be with me. If you aren't sure what to say, pray the *Padre Nuestro*. I find it calming and it helps evoke the presence of God.

Setting Up the Space

After cleaning/cleansing the room and yourself, you'll want to arrange your space. You should have a chair for the person to sit in, as well as a table or area cleared for the things you'll need. On the table you should have one white candle that is lit. This candle should have the cross carved into it, and you should pray the *Padre Nuestro* or the *Dios te Salve* over it three times before lighting. This candle represents the presence and purifying light of God. You should also have a bottle of Florida Water, a bottle of holy water, red ribbon, your bundles of herbs (for burning and for *barridas* if necessary), a small dish of salt, three eggs, and anything else you might feel you need. If you like to do smoke cleansing with a charcoal disk, make sure you have a heat-safe vessel and charcoal out and ready as well. I like to have a Bible on hand personally, but you'll find what you need the most.

You'll also want to wear some sort of personal protection. I wear a saint's medal and pray profusely beforehand for protection. You may use whatever you prefer; just know that it's best to wear some form of amulet. You are handling dangerous energies when doing a *limpia*, and you don't want them contaminating you as you work.

The Speedy Version

I'm a realistic person. Is it best if you clean your entire house and yourself thoroughly before attempting a *limpia*? Yes. Is it always practical? Absolutely not. Sometimes, your family busts in the door carrying your cousin Miguel, who was messing around in a cemetery and stepped on a bruja's *maleficio* and suddenly can't stay conscious and is vomiting profusely. Are you going to make them wait while you mop, shower, and set up your table? No. This is why it's good to keep your home clean in the first place, but in a pinch you can do what I call the "fast version."

To begin, light your white candle and drop some Florida Water into your palm and begin to rub your hands together as you start to pray profusely—this is important and we'll talk about why in a second. Make sure to also rub up to your elbows and get the back of your neck and over the top of your head with the Florida Water. I like to keep it in a spray bottle with some holy water and a small pinch of salt to just spray myself down real well, but work with what you have. Open a window and light up some cleansing herbs and begin to smoke the room, moving counterclockwise. This will help chase out anything evil, and then you can take the smoking herb bundle or resin to the person you are cleansing immediately after (more on that in a moment). Is this the best and most ideal way to go? No. Is this how we should approach all *limpias*? No. Is it effective and a good plan on short notice? Yes. Also be sure to thoroughly clean and cleanse your home after the work is done to ensure nothing is hiding amid the mess.

What's God Got to Do with It?

You may have noticed that a lot of this work requires prayer—not just any old prayer though, profuse and meaningful prayer! You see, the role of God is extremely important when it comes to *limpias*. The idea is that you are handling dark, dangerous, and evil energies that may wish to harm you and the person you are trying to help. You as a person alone are not strong enough to go against these beings. The one who is the strongest, though, and the one these energies and spirits fear the most is God. He is strong enough and can work through you. In Curanderismo, the *curanderos* are not the ones doing the work, they often channel powerful spirits, including God, to do the work through them. They are simply a conduit or vessel for holy power. Being energetically cleansed and healthy is important to this work because it keeps us a clear channel for God. That's why you should also never attempt this work after you've been drinking or using recreational drugs or are in poor health. You are not a good channel at those times.

When doing this work, it's important to keep a near constant stream of prayer going; remember this creates a bridge through which God can reach down and connect with us. You may pray words from the heart or repeat your favorite prayers such as the *Padre Nuestro*. You may ask for the help of saints, angels, Guadalupe, and ancestors as well as God, but God should be invoked most strongly and first. Pray with intensity. Pray like you mean it. Pray like you and the person you are helping depend on it—because you do.

Sahumerio

Sahumerio is a technical term for smoke cleansing. This is the act of burning herbs or resins either in bundles or on a charcoal disk. It's a great place to start because it not only helps to cleanse the room, but it is also a simple way to get to know a person's energy and their spirits and ease them into the session before you start whacking them with herbs. For this part of the cleansing, I like to use resins like white copal or frankincense. They are high vibrational but not so harsh that a person's energy or spirits might perceive it as an attack.

You see, all of us carry spirits with us. These are our ancestors, our guardian angels, and guides that are here to protect us. They may act as gatekeepers to this work and fight back if you come at the person you are working on too hard. The process of smoke cleansing helps to clear out any bad energy or evil spirits that may be residing around the person (in what most of us would call their aura), and it gives you a chance to make friends with their spirits. During this time I often say prayers, explaining who I am, what I plan to do, and why I'm going to be doing it. I clarify that I mean no harm and pray I am working in the highest good. I then ask permission. In almost every case the answer will be yes. However, if you suddenly feel like the answer is no, or you suddenly feel very anxious or like it's a bad idea, end the session immediately. For whatever reason, their spirits are making the call, and it's in everyone's best interest if you respect that.

Before you begin, remember to pray over the herbs and resins you will be using. Say your prayers for yourself as well and connect with God. Once you have your herbs or resins smoldering and the smoke wafting nicely, begin by making a short counter-clockwise circle around the person to dispel any bad spirits and come to stand behind them. I then start at the top of the head and gently blow the smoke over their crown. This is when I greet and introduce myself to their guardian spirits and begin to ask for permission. When I feel I have permission, I begin to work downward, just giving everything a good once over; repeat on the front.

Notice if there are places where the smoke suddenly begins to billow profusely or dies down. The areas where it begins to really smoke for seemingly no reason are the areas that will need the most attention; the places that barely smoke are not as bad. The spirits of the herbs and resins know. Take a breath and blow the smoke into the areas where it naturally billows to help break up the energy there. If they have anxiety or depression, blow the smoke over their forehead to chase away bad thoughts. I'll also do this at places where I feel they may have a blockage or places where they have chronic pain. This can help unblock the energy or at least loosen it up enough to be taken care of by a sweep later.

Barridas

The second type of *limpia* we will be covering is *barridas* or "sweeps." These are the most commonly recognized forms of *limpias.* This is the act of taking an object such as a bundle of herbs or an egg and sweeping the body downward with it. The idea is that negativity, sickness, hexes, as well as spiritual attachments, are swept away or collected by the object you are sweeping with. Just like cleaning the home, a person should also be cleansed top to bottom and back to front. All *barridas* begin at the top of the head and move down. Moving back up the body is considered redepositing the bad energy. Once you make your way from top to bottom, you may then return to the top and go down again, just don't run the object up their body; remove it completely and bring it to the top and begin once more. When you are done making your way down the body, be sure to get the bottoms of the feet and sweep them from heel to toe.

When doing *barridas* or *limpias* of any kind, it's important to pay special attention to the top of the head, back of the neck, between the shoulder blades, shoulders, palms of the hands, genitals, and soles of the feet. Now, in this day and age it's likely that you'll want to skip the genitals portion as it might get you arrested. However, if you know the person well, it is an important area to hit—especially if the person is suffering from reproductive problems. The genitals are the site of frequent magical attack from evil spell workers, and people tend to also hold a lot of trauma in their nether regions. Unless accommodations need to be made for sick or disabled folks, it's best for the person to stand during all *barridas*.

We will now discuss the different kinds of *barridas*, beginning with the *limpia con huevo*, because it is slightly different from the other methods.

Limpia con Huevo

Limpia con huevo or "cleansing with an egg" is the *limpia* most commonly seen in media and other representations of Curanderismo. While it has its limitations, it's frequently used to remove *Mal de Ojo*, sickness, minor hexes and curses, parasitic spirit attachments, and things like *envidias*, a type of spiritual poisoning caused by gossip and envy. When in doubt, *limpia con huevo*.

Eggs are a little different from other forms of *barridas* in that they absorb and contain the bad energy being removed where other forms sweep it away. This means that once the *limpia* is completed, you can crack the egg open and see what you are dealing with. A normal-looking yolk post-*limpia* indicates that there was not much wrong with the person. A yolk that comes out dark, bloody, or spotted indicates that spiritual sickness was absorbed into the egg, and depending on the severity, more *limpias* may be required. Before you start, you may want to wrap red ribbon around the hand that will be holding the egg to prevent anything from coming into you as you work.

To begin, take your egg in hand, and using some holy water, Florida Water, or an appropriate oil, make the sign of the cross on the egg. As you do this, begin to pray. Pray to God and ask that all evil, *brujería*, and sickness be removed from the person and drawn into "this most perfect, sacred, and holy vessel"— aka the egg. Beginning at the top of the head, and praying profusely, begin to make the sign of the cross or circles with the egg. Stay there until you feel the pull to move down to the forehead and begin making the sign of the cross there. The entire time you are doing this *limpia* you should be praying for freedom from evil energies and visualizing the egg sucking up all negativity like a powerful vacuum. In my mind I often see this as black smoke inside the person that's getting pulled out and trapped in the egg.

After making the sign of the cross on the brow several times— do it as long as you feel is necessary—I then pick up the egg, bring it back to the top of the head, and start rubbing it down the back of their head, getting behind the ears and coming to focus on the back of the neck where I begin to make the sign of the cross again. You may have to lift up their hair with your free hand as you do this. Stay there for as long as you need, praying that anything attached there gets removed. Then take the egg and glide it across each shoulder, removing the burdens of their life. Then travel down to the space between the shoulder blades, and make the sign of the cross here repeatedly, focusing on drawing out all evil and clearing any attached spirits.

The back of the neck and between the shoulder blades are especially important places because that is where spirits will attach. It's possible to have astral parasites, or what I call "wee beasties," crawling around the entire body, but ghosts and spirits will most often make a home here if they are going to feed on a person. So pay special attention to these places. Please note that depending on what you are dealing with, you may need a lot more than a *limpia con huevo,* so don't forget your protections and please reach out to a professional for guidance if you feel you are in over your head. This technique is mostly for collecting bad energy, such as *envidias, mal de ojo,* and hexes, but is not meant to absorb full spirits. Small entities or loose attachments may be cleared this way, but big stuff might need a different approach. As you work, keep a good grip on the egg and be prepared for anything. It's not uncommon for me to get the sudden mental image of a large spider or crab-like creature crawling out from somewhere inside the person and into the egg. Don't be alarmed if this happens to you too. This is just a spirit parasite getting removed. This is why you should have your hand wrapped in something red to protect yourself.

As you go, be very thorough, going down the back of the body to the heels. Most folks only need one, but if the egg begins to feel heavy or full, you may want to use a second or third egg depending on the severity of the case. Once you've made it down the back of the body, you'll want to start again on the front of the body. I revisit the brow, starting there and making the sign of the cross. I then move down the sides of the head, making the sign of the cross over each ear and traveling down the sides of the neck, coming to the heart center. There I pause and repeatedly make the sign of the cross. People hold a lot of stress and emotional trauma here, and it can take a while to work through—so take your time. From there I go down the arms and pause at the palms of the hands, where I also make the sign of the cross repeatedly.

I then return to the heart center and make my way down the torso—be mindful of sensitive or inappropriate areas and skip over sections of the body entirely if it's too intimate. Making your way down the legs, come to a stop at the feet and go across the soles from heel to toe and make the sign of the cross at least once on the bottom of both feet. Don't feel like you have to come in contact with every square inch of their body (that would be weird): just give them a good once over.

Once you are done, either immediately dispose of the egg, or crack it open to inspect the insides. I don't always look unless I know I'm working with something malefic or unusual and need to gauge the severity. If you can, take the egg outside the home immediately and dispose of it in the garbage. That is best. But again, do what is most practical. Just don't leave it in your home for long after the *limpia* is finished.

If you don't have an egg, there are a few alternative options. Some folks use limes (or lemons, if bad luck is involved), and I find these are excellent for a deep scrub where some cutting power is needed. In the case of removing harmful energy caused by gossip or *chisme,* you may want to use an alum crystal. When you are done, you can burn it on a charcoal disk and divine information about the person speaking ill of you in the melted remains. Black or white candles can also be used in a pinch to draw off and trap all kinds of nastiness. Once finished with the cleansing, burn the candle to completion, and throw out the leftover wax.

Limpia con Hierbas

Cleansing with herbs is the second most common type of *barrida* we will cover here. This is done in much the same way as the *limpia con huevo*, but it's slightly less complicated. To begin you'll need to make what we call an *escoba* or "broom." This is simply a bundle of fresh herbs tied together at the base. Usually these herbs are secured with red ribbon or string several inches from the bottom to create a handle, the idea being that the red ribbon acts as a barrier between your hand and the rest of *la escoba*, which will be coming in contact with the person you are cleansing. You still may want to wrap red ribbon around your hands or wrists when doing this though. Your *escoba* may be made of one type of plant or out of several different kinds (see page 129). Don't make it too complicated: between one and three plants in your bundles will be enough. Always be sure to tailor your selection to each person's individual needs. One person may need *ruda*, but the next might need *romero*. You may also use bunches of soft flowers like a bouquet of carnations or fragrant herbs such as lemon balm and mint. You'll get to know their unique properties as you use them. These powerful plant spirits make this type of *barrida* versatile and potent medicine.

Once you've made your *escoba*, you'll want to sprinkle it lightly with holy water and pray over it profusely. Continue to pray as you bring it with you to stand behind the person you are working on. Hold *la escoba* up to the sky and wait. Continue praying until you feel the connection to God form, then start your sweeping at the top of the head and work down the body. Sweeping with a bundle of herbs takes less time as they are often larger and cover more ground than a small egg. As you do this, remember to work downward and pray continuously for deliverance from evil and sickness. Visualize the herbs sweeping away anything bad or unhealthy from the person's body, spirit, and aura. Pay special attention to the back of the neck, shoulders, between the shoulder blades, heart center, genitals (if appropriate), the palms of the hands, and soles of the feet (heel to toe).

When you feel you are finished, take the *escoba* in hand and break it in half—since you should be using fresh plants, they may not break but simply bend; this is fine—symbolically splitting the bad energy and rendering it inert. Promptly throw it on the ground, or better yet, into the trash. Do not reuse *escobas*.

Baños

Baños or "baths" are frequently used water *limpias* designed to wash away bad spirits, malefic spells, and other unsavory energies. As a worker, you should never bathe a person—because, well, that's just weird. But baths may be prepared and sent home with the individual or, on occasion when I've worked with friends, done in a bathing suit. It should be said before we begin that these baths are not the fancy ones you see on Instagram. No, ma'am. These are real business. There are no crystals, bath bombs, or romance novels to read while you soak. Nope. These can be rather intense for some folks, especially if they are expecting a spa treatment. These baths are mostly used to strip off bad luck, bad spirits, and malefic witchcraft. There is no room for bubbles here. The person should also shower before the *baño*. You won't be getting clean in this type of bath: it's an in and out type of situation most of the time.

Usually these baths—especially the bitter ones—are mixed up in a bucket and poured over the person. They may opt to use a sponge or a cloth and soak it in the mix, squeeze over themselves, and wipe themselves down, which is fine. Just remember if it's a cleansing bath, it should all be done in a downward fashion. Others prefer to just pick it up and dump the whole thing on themselves. To each their own. Just make sure that they pray while they do it.

Either way, when the person takes the bath, they should light two white candles and place them on either end of the tub. This sets up a sort of screen or filter for the process so that when they leave the bath, they don't take anything bad with them. The candles should be blessed and have a cross carved in them. The person bathes in their preferred method then exits the tub. The method of drying depends on the type of bath. Some say towel-drying is fine; others require air-drying and can be very uncomfortable, but sometimes you have to suffer for what you want.

Bitter Bath

The bitter bath is the most unpleasant but also the most helpful kind. Bitter baths cut through blockages and bad energy and cleanse the person. These baths are often served cold. It's the medicine you need, not necessarily the medicine you want.

To make your bitter bath, you'll need to select your herbs. Take into consideration the problems the person is facing when making your selection and choose accordingly. I will add some recipe suggestions below. Once you have your herbs, you will want to pray over them and ask them for their help with whatever issues are being faced. Then get a bucket or a large bowl and fill it with cool water. Spring water is best, but work with what you have. Bless the water by making the sign of the cross over it and praying the *Padre Nuestro*, then add in your fresh herbs.

For this method it's best to use fresh herbs; we'll discuss dried herbs below. With both hands, reach into the water and begin to pray. As you pray for healing and cleansing, begin to work the plants in your hands. Squeeze them and tear them up gently but firmly, really getting them mixed in well. Do this for several minutes to infuse the water with prayer and the power of the plants. You should have enough plant matter in the bowl that it looks like soup when you are done. Generally speaking I use one large handful of each plant, or if I'm using only one plant, I use three handfuls of it.

If you have only dried herbs to work with, you'll want to approach things a little differently. I make a long infusion. First, I select the herbs I want to work with and pray over them while adding three spoonfuls of each to a quart-sized mason jar. I then fill the jar with boiling water and carefully cap it. Do *not* shake the mixture and be careful handling it—it's very hot. I let it sit in the fridge for at least four hours or until all the plant matter settles to the bottom. Remember, it should be cold when you go to use it. This essentially creates a very strong tea that I add to a bucket with cool water and anything else I might need to include. If you have both fresh and dried plant matter you can do both, and add the cool infusion to the water with the fresh plants in it.

If you prefer to soak in the mixture for some reason, or the person you are working with just can't wrap their head around the bucket situation, you may dump whichever version you have made into a regular bathtub full of water and soak in it. It's a bit diluted this way but should still be effective. In a pinch you can simply boil the herbs in a pot for ten to twenty minutes before straining into bath water.

Bath to Remove *Mal de Ojo* and Malefic Witchcraft

If you fear you have been given *Ojo* by someone or that someone has worked a curse on you, this simple bath will help take it off.

You'll need:

Rue
Agrimony
1 handful blessed salt
Laundry bluing (for Ojo*)*

Make this bath in your preferred manner depending on if you have fresh or dried plants, and add the bluing at the end. Laundry bluing is an old household product and can be found next to the laundry detergent. The color blue is often considered in cultures throughout the world as both a protection and a cure for *Ojo*. Blot dry with a towel when done.

Bath to Remove Evil Spirits

Sometimes we pick up a spiritual hitchhiker of sorts. These are ghosts or entities that attach to us and try to feed off our energy. This can be alarming when it happens, but not to worry, it is easily remedied with the right plants.

You'll need:

Espanta muerto
Rue
Garlic
Salt (blessed)

I prefer to make this bath with about a quarter cup salt, and fresh garlic when available (it's easiest to use when minced or pressed). Yes, you will smell funny, but it will do the trick. Pray the *Padre Nuestro* over the *baño* three times and continue to pray as you bathe. Be sure to get the top of your head and the back of your neck really well. This is one that you will want to air-dry for.

Bath to Remove Bad Luck
We all have bad luck sometimes. We have bad days—or even bad weeks. However, sometimes it seems like more than that, like we've stepped in something and can't shake it. In that case, we'll need to strip it off you like paint.

You'll need:

> *1 pint white vinegar*
> *Lemon peels*
> *Parsley*

This one I like to make ahead of time in a pint-size mason jar. I add in the vinegar and lemon peels and let it sit for at least three hours (overnight is best). I then add it to a bucket with the cool water with the fresh parsley and work it all together with prayer. This will strip all your bad luck and give you a fresh start (see the Law of Replacement section on page 158). If your luck is really terrible, you may want to use ammonia in place of vinegar. *Do not* use a full pint of ammonia in this bath; use three to seven *drops*! I use a medicine dropper for this, and I recommend you wear gloves when handling it. Ammonia is extremely powerful and can burn you if applied directly to the skin. Use only miniscule amounts diluted in large amounts of water, and avoid getting in the eyes and mouth. When you use ammonia, you won't strip just bad luck but good luck as well. This is a hard reset and only should be used only in dire circumstances. Rinse off in the shower afterward, and towel dry when finished.

Sweet Baths

Sweet baths are much more pleasant than bitter baths. They are generally served warm and contain flowers and other more luxurious ingredients. These are not stripping the way that bitter baths are and are often employed to soothe or to place another layer on top of something. Think of them as less of an antiseptic, and more of a salve or balm.

Sweet baths are made the same way as bitter ones, with prayer and intention as you work the materials into the water. Some sweet baths use milk as a base instead of water, but more commonly it is are just added into the water as an ingredient. Also if employing dried ingredients, the infusions don't have to be refrigerated beforehand. They may be left at room temperature until you need them. These types of baths function as a balm for all kinds of issues such as heartbreak, frayed nerves, and self-esteem problems. These need to be fixed, but not necessarily cleansed away. I often make up these baths in a large bowl and then pour them into a warm bath in a bathtub. However, if you prefer the bucket method, by all means go for it.

Bath for Heartbreak

When suffering from a broken heart, it can feel as if the entire world is falling apart. We can't breathe. We can't eat or even think clearly. To ease this pain, use the following bath.

You'll need:

1 handful pink carnations
1 handful fresh lavender
1 sprig fresh rosemary
1 can coconut milk
1 pint hawthorn infusion

In a large bowl or a bucket of warm water, work all the ingredients together with prayer and intention. Pray for healing and for soothing of the broken heart. I like to pray Psalm 23 into these as well because it brings peace to the soul. After mixing, pour into a warm bath and soak in the mixture for twenty minutes. Blot dry with a towel afterward.

Psalm 23

The Lord is my shepherd; I shall not want.

He maketh me to lie down in green pastures: he leadeth me
  beside the still waters.

He restoreth my soul: he leadeth me in the paths of
  righteousness for his name's sake.

Yea, though I walk through the valley of the shadow of
  death, I will fear no evil: for thou art with me; thy rod
  and thy staff they comfort me.

Thou preparest a table before me in the presence of mine
  enemies: thou anointest my head with oil; my cup
  runneth over.

Surely goodness and mercy shall follow me all the days
  of my life; and I will dwell in the house of the Lord
  for ever.

Bath for Self-Love

One of the most common spells folks ask me for is for self-love. This is an area where a lot of people struggle. Sometimes the hardest person to love is ourselves, but that doesn't mean we shouldn't try.

You'll need:

2 sweet cinnamon sticks
1 orange

1 handful pink rose petals
1 cup pineapple juice

Begin by crushing up the cinnamon sticks into small pieces and peeling the orange. Chop up the orange peels into small pieces and squeeze the orange juice into a glass. Once you're done, add everything to a bowl of warm water. Work them together with prayer and intention and add the mixture to a warm bath. Soak for twenty minutes. Blot dry with a towel afterward.

Bath for Frayed Nerves

Sometimes we are at the end of our rope. We may be feeling stressed over our job, our family, or the world at large, but there comes a time where we feel we constantly are on the verge of tears—if not a full breakdown—and we just need a rest. For this I recommend the following bath. It might not fix the whole world, but it might talk you down off the ledge.

You'll need:

1 large handful lavender flowers
1 quart chamomile infusion
1 can coconut milk
1 handful oats
1 handful Epsom salts (optional)

Work all ingredients together in warm water with prayer and intention and pour them into a warm bath. Soak for at least fifteen minutes, and blot dry. This is best done right before bed.

Fire Limpias

Fire *limpias* are a powerful class of *limpias* generally dedicated to cleansing both the spirit and the space. Any technique that uses a flame falls into this category, including the candle sweep we talked about in the *barridas* section. Because of this, these tend to be the most dangerous type of cleansing and therefore the most infrequently used. Make sure to practice good sense and take proper safety precautions when attempting any of these.

We'll discuss two techniques in this section: the candle flame *limpia* and the white fire *limpia*. Both utilize the purifying and transformational power of fire. In most traditions backed by Christianity, the element of fire is representative of *El Espíritu Santo* (the Holy Spirit). This makes it an excellent element for lifting and removing the heavy stuff.

Candle Flame Limpia

For this *limpia* you will need one white candle that has been cleansed and blessed. I prefer to use a glass-encased novena for this. With stick candles you risk wax drip and mess depending on where the cleansing is done. A novena that's been burned down just a couple inches is ideal because it won't drip wax and the glass adds an extra layer of safety between the flame and the person.

This technique is not generally used for a full body cleanse the way that *baños* and *barridas* are. We use this *limpia* for specific areas of trouble only, like a spot treatment, because it can break up areas of heavy energy and blockages in the energy system.

To begin, take your cleansed and blessed candle in hand and with your finger, make the sign of the cross on the glass with holy water. As you do this, begin to pray and light the candle.

Take the burning candle to the problem areas, and while saying prayers for healing and freedom from sickness and evil, make the sign of the cross above the afflicted area with the flame. Make sure you are doing this *above* the area and not on the skin. I like to visualize the flame leaving a trail of brilliant white light marking the sign of the cross in the air, which remains there. Repeat this several times to reinforce the blessing, and then move on to the next area or set the candle aside. I prefer to let the candle burn all the way down after I've completed this *limpia* as a way of continuing to energize the work over time, but follow your instincts on this one.

White Fire Limpia

A white fire *limpia* is a powerful spiritual cleanser! This is used to cleanse a room or a home of all negative energy. It's also helpful if the person you are working with has a lot of heavy things they want to get off their chest and need to verbally dump out all of their issues. This is a very specific form of exorcism, where the person verbalizes their fear and regret and sins or whatever it is that they need to finally get out of themselves. This gives them a place to send it as they are speaking so that the person listening does not have to absorb it.

To start you'll need a heat-safe dish, a handful of salt, and alcohol. One option is to use Epsom salts and rubbing alcohol, and many people prefer this set of ingredients. However, I like to use sea salt and Florida Water. Place the salt in the dish and pour a bit of alcohol onto it—just enough to saturate the salt but not so much that it's a hazard. With a match or a lighter, ignite the alcohol and, voilà, you have your white fire *limpia*.

This may be placed in the center of the room on the floor or a table to cleanse the space of all negativity. It can also be carefully carried from room to room and left to sit for just a minute or so before moving on to the next—which is powerful way to cleanse your entire home.

Alternatively the unlit bowl may be set on a table between you and the person you are working with, particularly when that person needs to go through the verbal release I've described. Let them put into words all they need to get out as you witness but don't absorb what they are saying—simply let the words hang in the air. And then when they are done, ask them if they are ready to begin anew. When they say yes and agree to start fresh and make the necessary changes in their life, have them light the fire and cleanse away their words, fears, regrets, and past self. This purifies the room, you, and them to start a new life fresh and clean.

The Session

You may be feeling a little overwhelmed with all these different types of cleansings and wondering which to use. As you gain practice, you'll begin to know instinctually which ones are best to use for the person you are helping. However, as a beginner it's nice to have a bit of an outline to follow. Please understand that there is no set step-by-step procedure that will fit everyone's needs, and you should expect to tailor your approach to each individual. That being said, here is a basic outline to follow.

1. Begin by having a discussion with them about why they are there. This will help you gauge what it is you are dealing with. Some will be there just for the experience; others will have major issues. If they describe something to you that you are unprepared to handle, please do not go forward. Refer them to a professional instead.

2. *Sahumerio* is a great place to start. It gives you an opportunity to speak to their spirits and helps clean the room and their aura of negativity.

3. *Un limpia con huevo* can help you assess how bad the problem you are facing really is. Some folks won't be bad at all; others will be a mess.

4. From here you have some choices to make: *Sahumerio* again? *Una barrida con hierbas?* Maybe a *baño?* It will all depend on what you've been able to learn from what they've told you and what the egg looks like. Listen to your intuition as well: what is it telling you?

5. When you feel you've done your best, finish with something uplifting. (See "The Law of Replacement" below.)

Limpias and Children

Children's energy is very tender and often quite sensitive. Everything for children should be dialed back several notches. Most *barridas* will be fine, but I would use things like rose water instead of Florida Water, and *escobas* made of carnations instead of scratchy plants like *romero.* I'd also choose some sweet or gentle-smelling incense instead of something harsh. Their parents should be in the room, but try to talk to the child like an active participant, because they are. Explain in language they will understand what you are about to do so they know. This can be very scary for them, so be sure to be gentle, move slowly, and keep an open line of communication with them.

The Law of Replacement

When we are engaged in cleansings, we need to keep in mind an important point that is frequently overlooked: the Law of Replacement. Nature abhors a vacuum. This means if you remove something, there will be empty space that needs to be filled. If you don't actively choose to fill it with what you want, whatever happens to be floating by at the moment will move into the void, and then you are at the mercy of energetic roulette. This is never a good idea.

It's best to bless and fill the space with something good after something has been cleansed away.

For instance, if you are having bad luck and decide to strip away all your luck, it's important to then anoint with a Good Luck oil or take a good luck bath to fill that space with positive things! Otherwise, you leave it up to the whims of fate which way your luck will go, and it may go straight downhill and possibly be worse than before. So every time you do any type of cleansing where something is removed, always follow up with something to bring in good energies to replace it.

When we do this, we want to go the opposite direction we went when cleansing. For instance, if I'm working with a person who has gone through one hell of a cleansing, I will then anoint them with an oil—or have them do it themselves, so it's not weird. I would have them put a few drops of oil on their hands and rub them together while praying and then apply it to their body starting at the soles of the feet going toe to heel, and then up the body all the way to the crown of the head. Don't use enough to make them greasy; just a few drops will do. This helps draw the blessings up into the body. The same goes for the home: if we are bringing something into the home, we go from front door to back door and bottom floor to top floor.

Here are some ideas to get you started when it comes to bringing good things into the home through cleaning. Any of the sweeps may be sprinkled across the carpet and vacuumed up if that is what you have to work with.

Happy Home Sweep

After a deep home cleanse you may want to bring in happy home energy to fill the void. Blend together cinnamon sticks, cloves, lavender, and oats that you've prayed over in your mortar and pestle. Work them until the cinnamon sticks are down to small chips. Place this mix in your front doorway and sweep it into your home, all the way through and to your back door. I would also light some good-smelling incense while you do this.

Lucky Floor Sweep

To bring luck into the home, mix together cloves, dried five-finger grass, and dried eucalyptus that you've prayed over in your mortar and pestle. Sprinkle this at the front door and sweep it into the home toward the back door.

Love Floor Wash

If you are looking to get rid of bad luck in love, I recommend doing a salt sweep by sprinkling herbs like agrimony, rosemary, lemon balm, and/or hyssop that you've prayed over first across your floors. Sweep this out of the front door to cleanse away the negativity and to start new. Then do the following floor wash.

You'll need:

2 cinnamon sticks
1 handful cloves

1 handful rose petals
1 orange peel

Pray over these materials and then boil them together for ten to twenty minutes. Strain and add the liquid to a mop bucket half full of tepid water and your preferred detergent. Starting at the front door, mop into the home and finish at the back door. Throw the mop water out the back door and into the backyard to set it.

Protection Floor Wash

After a deep cleanse it's always great to then bring in protection to make sure nothing comes along and undoes your hard work.

You'll need:

1 handful cloves
1 pinch rue
1 spoonful angelica root

Pray over the herbs and boil them together for ten to twenty minutes. Strain and pour the liquid into a bucket half full of tepid water and your favorite detergent. Mop your home moving from front door to back door and then toss the mop water out the back door to set the work. Your home is now protected from evil spirits and *brujería*.

A Note of Caution

We live in turbulent times, and ideas around sexual harassment, consent, and personal boundaries are all hot button issues right now. When doing *limpias*, I highly recommend keeping an open line of communication with the person you are working with about what you plan to do and what they may experience as you do it. This is helpful in two ways. First it will let the person relax. Don't just come at them with a bundle of herbs and start smacking them to cast the demons out. Tell them what you plan to do and get their consent before you continue. Also ask them ahead of time if there are any places on their body that they don't want touched. Sometimes people have medical issues concealed under their clothes that you might stumble upon by accident. The second thing this informed consent does is make the *limpia* easier for the worker. If your subject is scared or tense, their energy will fight you—or worse their personal protective spirits may perceive you as a threat and attack.

If you plan to give *limpias* on a regular basis, it's also best to have someone with you as an assistant/witness in case there are any misunderstandings. If you don't speak Spanish, this assistant should be able to translate between you and the person you are working with to avoid any miscommunications or embarrassing situations. This goes for both men and women, but I recommend women especially do not see clients without anyone else around, as this can become a dangerous situation very quickly.

8

Hechizos

In this chapter we will be covering the art of *hechizos* or spells. These are simple works that are done with intention to bring about change or to fortify ourselves in some way. Most American Brujeria revolves around protection and the removal of evil, but there are a few tricks for other needs as well. Though deceptively simple, when approached the right way, these rituals can be extremely powerful.

The Art of Spellcasting

The number one thing required for spellcasting is faith. If you don't believe that what you are doing will help you, then it won't. Our faith in God and our work is what fuels this magic. If you don't believe that you are strong enough or magical enough to cast a spell, then believe that God or *La Virgen* is powerful enough and, through them, you are supported and able to do the work. After all, our connection to the divine is what makes the work happen, but we'll get to that in a moment. First, let's go through the steps.

Forming Your Intention

When casting a spell, the first thing you have to do is map out your intention. What is it that you want? If you don't know what you want, you'll never be able to get it. Be very clear when you form your intention. Maybe you want protection—but from what? I always recommend writing down your intention to start. Some of you will be long-winded and have a whole paragraph, but try to pare it down to one or two sentences if you can. Also, make sure that you are asking for only one thing. People will try to load three or four intentions into one spell, and that just never works out. An example of a good clear intention is, "I am protected from all evil spells and magical mischief." It's simple and clear. Also notice that it is in present tense and confident. Those two things are important as well. Once you have your intention, we can begin the work.

Selecting Your Materials

Most of the spells included in this book come with suggested materials, but if you are looking to cast a spell of your own, the task of selecting materials can be very daunting! How do you know what to choose? The main advice I can give you here is simple is always better. A lot of new workers try to make something really powerful by adding in a hundred different ingredients and making the spell super complicated. Juggling all these factors only detracts from the focus you should be putting into what you want. If you are in doubt, start with a simple candle. Use a white candle or a candle that is a color that represents your desire. (See *Las Velas* chapter.) You can use the list of herbs below or find reference books full of herbs and their magical uses—which can be extremely helpful when you are beginning. Remember your herbs can be used however you would like and in whatever way makes sense to you. For instance, you may take a protective herb like rosemary and sprinkle it in a circle around a red candle for protection—simple and effective. You may also choose incense sticks that match your intention, such as Love or Romance incense for a love spell. Before you know it, you have put together a candle, some herbs, and incense. That is a spell—especially once you add in the divine as we'll discuss below! Just remember, it's very hard to do a spell wrong as long as the steps you are taking make sense in your mind and your intention is clear.

Remember that when you are doing your spell, you are showing God/Guadalupe what you want through symbols. So if you are trying to separate two things, burn a candle for each and set them far apart, or put an object like a brick between them. If you are trying to bring two things together, burn a candle for each and place them close together, or even tie them together with string before you light them. If you'd like to cut out a bad habit, burn a candle to represent the habit that has been anointed with banishing oil, or burn the candle in the open jaws of a pair of sharp scissors. As long as it's simple and makes sense, you should be good to go.

Connecting to La Virgen

After you've prepared your space—cleansing is always a good idea—and gathered your materials, you'll want to bring in the divine. This is how magic happens. We channel the divine into our mundane objects and lives in order to create something we want. To do this, we pray. Yup, prayer—I told you this would be important and you've seen it time and time again through this book. Pray like you mean it. Pray like it's important, because it is. When we pray with intensity, we pull *La Virgen,* God, or a saint (whichever you choose to work with) down to us where they can listen. We pray over our tools to bring the holy power of the divine into them, transforming them from simple objects into powerful instruments of the change! We pray and speak our intention so that God or *La Virgen* knows what it is that we want. We state it clearly so that they understand. We then spell it out further by showing in symbols what we want by performing a spell. The lit red candle is a symbol of protection. The circle of protective herbs around the candle is another symbol of protection. Our prayers asking for protection as well reinforce this message to God.

Once you have all of these in place, you must remember to have faith! Even if your spell is simple, even if it's just placing a pair of scissors in your windowsill—be intentional about why you are doing it and *know* that the work is powerful and will accomplish what you need it to. After all, our ancestors have been doing this work for a long time, and we wouldn't still be doing it if it didn't work!

Magical Timing

Almost all schools of magic follow at least one indicator of magical timing. Magical timing is an idea that suggests certain times of day, week, or month are better for certain types of spells. This doesn't mean that we can't do spells at any time: we can and should do them when we need them regardless of the time of day or phase of the moon. However, if we are able to line up our magic with special timing, then it just adds a little extra power. Think of it like making cookies. If you use just any flour, the cookies will probably turn out just fine. But if you use the good flour, they'll turn out even better. Either way you'll have results, but following magical timing can help make them even better. There are two main ways to do this and we'll discuss both.

Days of the Week

Each day of the week is ruled by a planetary sign that indicates what kind of work it's good for. For instance, Monday is ruled by the moon. This makes it a great day for psychic and intuitive work. It's also a good day for meditation and other receptive mental/intuitive work as well as spells for fertility.

Tuesday is ruled by Mars. Mars is the planet of war and action. Spells for protection and the creation of defensive charms are best done on this day, as are reversals, works of aggression, and domination.

Wednesday is ruled by Mercury. This is the best day to do works regarding your career or job-related issues. Mercury is a thoughtful and ambitious planet, and this makes Wednesday a good day for study and works concerning the mind and schooling. Travel planning or spells concerning travel are also best done on this day.

Thursday is ruled by Jupiter. This energy deals well with matters of money and personal finance. Prosperity spells are especially effective when cast on this day. Jupiter also rules over legal and governmental issues, so magic concerning court proceedings or immigration are best done on this day.

Friday is ruled by Venus. Venus is the planet associated with love and sensuality. Spells for beauty, romance, love, sex, attraction, glamour, and feminine power get extra zing on Friday. Reconciliation spells to bring a lost lover back are best done on Fridays.

Saturday is ruled by Saturn. This is the day for stripping away all negative or unhelpful influences before the start of the new week. This means spells to aid weight loss, cut ties with toxic family members, and very similar, overcoming addiction are best done on this day. Saturday is also the day for cursing, hexing, reversals, banishing, and binding.

Sunday is the most powerful day and ruled by the sun. All works can be done on Sunday, especially those that are benevolent or for the greater good. This especially includes works of healing, blessing, and protecting. In my experience, road-opening spells are particularly effective when done on Sundays, as well as any works that relate to angels or saints.

The Moon

Most forms of folk magic don't follow the lunar influence because it's considered "witchcraft." Though we know that folk magic and witchcraft are very similar, to our ancestors there was a big difference. Still, in American Brujeria it's common to take lunar timing into account when working your *hechizos*.

The new moon is the phase that confuses most people when they get introduced to lunar timing. You see, astronomically the new moon is the day in which the moon is completely black. In magic, we refer to this as the "dark moon." In magical timing the "new moon" is the day following the dark moon, when the smallest, faintest sliver is visible. When the new moon is in the sky, it's a good time to begin things, like spells to start a new job or bring in a new love. Fertility work is best done at this time as well.

The waxing moon is the section of time—generally two weeks—where the moon grows from crescent to full. This is the time to grow things or bring things in. Works for love, manifesting, healing, and protection are good to do during this time.

When the moon is full, it is at its most powerful. This is the time to seize what you want! Remember, during the full moon we are still bringing in what we want. We may also do works to illuminate situations by bringing in the truth. Powerful works of justice are also most effective at this time.

Just after the full moon, the waning phase begins, which lasts for about two weeks. This is the phase in which the moon shrinks from full all the way back to being completely black. As the moon disappears, it's a time to make other things disappear. Works of banishing, cleansing, releasing, and removal are best done during this phase.

When the moon returns to its completely black state—the dark moon—it's an excellent time for binding, banishing, and hex work. Consider this period for cutting ties with toxic people and ending relationships that are unhealthy. This is the time to work any magic concerning hiding, invisibility, secrets, and the dead.

Herbal Allies

When learning to cast spells of any kind, it's important to get familiar with some of the more useful herbal allies. While this book does not serve as a complete guide to herbal magic, it's always nice to have a list available for quick reference.

Abre camino: Literally translates to "open roads" and is used to clear your life path of obstacles.

Agrimony: Good for removing hexes and curses and sending them back to the caster.

Anise: This herb helps bring in luck and money but has a special affinity for opening the psychic senses and raising vibrations.

Bay: Helps with luck, brings victory/success, imparts protection, and draws money.

Black pepper: Repels enemies, gives body to hexes, and creates a strong protective wall against evil.

Camphor: Raises vibrations, banishes evil, brings in good spirits.

Carnations: These flowers add extra power to spells.

Catnip: Attracts lovers and increases luck.

Cinnamon: Brings in luck, money, and success in business. It's a famous love plant, but can also be protective and cleansing when burned. Added to spells it can speed up their results.

Cloves: Brings in luck, money, success, and good business, and warms relationships. This plant also imparts protection from evil, stops gossip, and has mildly dominating properties.

Coffee: The grounds or beans added to spells increase their energy, speed, and vigor. It can be used to cause nervousness in your enemies or be brewed into cups that are added to baths to remove bad luck, hexes, and other spells and energies.

Fennel: Keeps the law away.

Five-finger grass: Also known as cinquefoil, this plant brings in all manner of luck and opportunities! It's also good at breaking hexes, especially those affecting your luck.

Garlic: Drives away all evil, exorcises negative spirits, and clears sickness. Garlic is sacred to St. Michael.

Hyssop: A deeply cleansing herb that removes curses, negativity, sin, and more! Bathe with hyssop after curse work.

Lavender: Brings peace and tranquility to any situation. Can be used in love spells to quiet quarreling or to calm a nervous target. It also has a great ability to ward off evil and bring in good luck. Lavender is considered lightly dominating.

Lemon balm: Clears away hexes affecting your love life, brings in good luck, and opens roads.

Lemons: Cut through negativity and can "sour" a situation. These are also used to clean up bad luck and restore good fortune.

Limes: Cut through negativity and can bind the mouth, bringing a halt to gossip and lies.

Nutmeg: Attracts love (especially from men), warms relationships, and draws in prosperity.

Orange: Orange peel imparts courage, love, hope, and open roads.

Oregano: Keeps away meddling/bothersome individuals and/or those who might turn you over to the authorities.

Red pepper: Red pepper is used for protection and for causing confusion and/or anger in enemies.

Rose: This is the queen of all flowers and imparts confidence, superiority, and protection to those with feminine energy. She is also one of the best herbs at bringing in love, romance, and commitment.

Rosemary: This herb drives off evil and is used to fight all kinds of negative energy. Grown by the door it protects the home. Rosemary is good for relieving depression and strengthening mental powers such as memory and clarity.

Sulfur: Used in works both good and evil. When burned, it chases away evil spirits. Added to candles, it removes obstacles and crosses enemies.

Thyme: This herb brings in money and prosperity!

Vervain: All vervain is considered equal, but I prefer blue vervain. Vervain is used for all things! It brings in luck and blessings. It opens roads, breaks hexes, protects fiercely, and heals broken love. Truly, when you don't know what to use, try vervain.

Crafting Your Own Oils

I love shopping for condition oils at the botanica! There are so many fun ones to choose from, and they each have their own unique properties and uses. However, an unsettling number of these special oils are no more than artificial coloring and perfume. I hate to say it, but most of these are a scam and don't hold much real power. When shopping for oils, always check to make sure that there are at least some leaves, roots, or stones inside. If there aren't any, then it's a good chance that oil isn't going to help you. After all, where is its power coming from if there's nothing in it? So what can we do? We make our own.

Base Oils

To begin, you will have to choose from a selection of base oils. I know many people like to use almond oil, but it can be pricey. Olive oil is a classic favorite, but olive oil has a tendency to go rancid more quickly than others. It also has a distinct scent and color. Coconut oil can be fun because at certain temperatures it's in a solid state and can be applied to the candle or body like a salve. However, coconut oil has a strong scent that you'll have to compete with. I personally like sunflower oil—relatively no scent, mostly clear in color, and it won't break the bank. If you feel fancy, you may add vitamin E to your oils to extend their shelf life.

Selecting and Processing Ingredients

The next thing you'll need to do is pick your plants and other items that will go in the oil. All plants that are added to oils should be dried. If you add fresh plant matter to your oils, it will go rancid. Choose just a few herbs that will contribute to your intent. Pray over each herb and ask it to help you toward your goal with its own unique properties, then add it to your mortar and pestle. Once you've chosen and prayed over all your herbs, grind them together while praying for what it is you want—really pull God down into the mortar with your prayers. Once finished, add these plants to a dry sterile jar. You may also add objects such as crystals, holy medals, nails, written prayers, animal teeth, coins, string, chain links, or anything else that will contribute to your purpose. Be sure to pray over these objects as well. Once they are all in the jar, fill it to the top with your oil.

You may also scent your oil with essential oils. However, I do not recommend substituting oil for whole plants if you can help it. This happens far too often in modern witchcraft, and it's not as effective. We must also remember that these condition oils are not meant to be perfumes, so if we leave them unscented, they will still be just as powerful. Still, I have noticed that the first thing people do when they open an oil is smell it, and they often look disappointed if there's no scent. So I add a light scented agent to most of my oils and find that this contributes to the overall experience of using them. Just don't go overboard. When you're done, put the lid on the jar and make sure it's screwed on tight.

"Cookin'" the Oil

Once your jar is sealed, I recommend a spiritual cooking process. I say "spiritual cooking" because we aren't going to really apply more than gentle heat to the oil; it's more about infusing the oil with the energy of the plants. This helps it all marinate together into a more complete unit.

You'll need:

Your jar full of oil
1 small white plate
5 white tea lights
1 rosary
1 Sharpie

To begin, shake your jar full of oil while praying profusely for the blessings of God and for the oil to be infused with the power, energy, and intention it needs. Place the jar on the white plate and surround it closely with four white tea lights in a cross pattern—also on the plate if there's room. Place the fifth tea light on the lid of the jar. Light the four base lights in the name of the Holy Trinity, and as you light the top one, pray the *Padre Nuestro* over the whole setup. You may also pray words from the heart or the *Dios te Salve* over the setup as well. This act of burning the tea lights around the jar is a way of feeding the oils, energizing them with light. Also if the candles are close to the jar—I use mason jars because they are heat-safe—the flames gently warm the oil to help the actual plant parts infuse. Once the candles are lit, I like to place my rosary around the plate as a means of concentrating the power and protecting the oil from outside energies that might contaminate it.

Once the candles are done burning, you may use the oil immediately or repeat the candle-burning step for multiple days in a row. It's ready to go after one round, but the more times you repeat the feeding process, the stronger it will be. Either way, as soon as the first round is done, mark the jar with the sign of the cross using the Sharpie to seal in the power and protect it from being contaminated by outside energies. You may also want to write what type of oil is in the jar so you don't forget.

Other folks skip this process entirely and place the oil in a mason jar and set that in a saucepan with an inch or two of water to gently heat it for about thirty minutes. This does a good job of infusing, but it takes a bit more finesse and isn't quite as ceremonial. It's easy to overheat or underheat the oil, and each type reacts differently to temperature, so read your labels carefully.

Recipes

Blessing Oil
You'll need:

> *1 small unopened bottle of olive oil*
> *Salt (blessed)*

Open the new bottle and add in a small pinch of blessed salt. Then pray the *Padre Nuestro* into the bottle three times, followed by Psalm 23 (see page 152). Cap the bottle and use anytime you need to bless candles or objects with holy power.

Love Oil
You'll need:

> *Rose petals*
> *Cinnamon chips*
> *Lavender*

Follow the instructions given above to mix the herbs and cook the oil. Use this oil to anoint candles for love spells as well as gifts and notes to your beloved. Added to your perfume or cologne it helps create an aura of romance.

Money Oil

You'll need:

> *Cloves*
> *Cinnamon*
> *Five-finger grass*

Mix the herbs and cook the oil. Use this oil to anoint money candles as well as the money in your wallet to help it grow. Add it to perfume or cologne when going to a job interview.

Protection Oil

You'll need:

> *Rue*
> *Cloves*
> *Black peppercorns*

Mix the herbs and cook the oil. Use this oil to anoint protection candles, amulets, your car, and/or your body when you need protection.

Deliverance Oil

You'll need:

> *Agrimony*
> *Rue*
> *White clover flowers*

Mix the herbs and cook the oil. Add this oil to hand soap, shampoo, and/or body wash to wash away hexes that have been cast on you. You can also add this to baths and floor washes or anoint the body directly.

Psychic Oil

You'll need:

> *Anise*
> *Rosemary*
> *Cloves*

Mix the herbs and cook the oil. Use this oil to anoint your forehead and temples before beginning psychic work.

Road-Opening Oil

You'll need:

> Abre camino *(or vervain)*
> *Five-finger grass*
> *Lemon balm*
> *An old key*

Mix the herbs and cook the oil. Use this handy oil to anoint road-opening novenas or add it to perfume or cologne to increase opportunities.

Bibliomancy

All spiritual workers should have at least one form of divination they are comfortable with. We spoke about divination by reading a candle flame and glass earlier, but what about for everyday things? How do we receive messages from God and our ancestors outside of our dreams and feelings? One of the easiest ways I know is through bibliomancy—the art of divining information using the Bible. By selecting an excerpt while under divine guidance, we can receive messages from God and insight into our daily lives and our troubles.

To begin, take your Bible in hand and balance it on its spine on a desk or table. Close your eyes and begin to pray profusely, asking God, a saint, or the ancestors for guidance. If you have a particular question, make sure it's included as part of your prayer. As you continue to pray with your eyes closed, let go of the book and let it naturally fall open. Place your finger on the page and move it slowly over the text until you feel guided to stop. Once you've reached that place, open your eyes and read the passage. Sometimes shockingly accurate or insightful things can be divined using this method. If the Bible doesn't open to a page but continues to close itself after a couple tries, you are not meant to know the answer to that question.

An alternative method is to fan through the pages until you feel the need to stop. Then with eyes closed, randomly place your finger somewhere on the page and read what is written there. In either method if the passage doesn't immediately seem to make sense, I've found that reading further down the page often brings the message into focus. Also, sometimes it's not so much the exact words but the tone of the verse. If the verse does not make sense at all, that's an indication that the message is not willing to come through and you may not be allowed to know at this time.

La Brujería de Vicks VapoRub

Each one of us probably has a story about how our *abuelitos* loved and upheld the unparalleled healing power that is Vicks VapoRub. This is common among our people, but I have to say that my great grandma Lena Gonzales may have taken the gold medal for creative uses for Vicks "VapoRu," as she called it. Have a headache? She'd tell you to put it on your head. Have a stomachache? Put it on your stomach. Can't sleep? She'd put it on your eyelids. No, really, she'd put it on your eyelids. She'd also put it on your hands before bed to discourage masturbation—but that's another topic entirely.

I do *not* recommend putting Vicks on your eyelids or any other sensitive areas—that's a bad idea. But my Grandma Lena was a bit of a wild card. The woman kept plastic crabs on top of her fridge. She was also known to run out of her house screaming in Spanish and brandishing a carving knife if someone was on her lawn. One time some of my uncles got lice and she sprayed their heads with Raid. Clearly she's not someone you'd want to take medical advice from. Still, her absolute faith and commitment to the powers of Vicks VapoRub have inspired me to share this section in hopes that it reminds you of your own crazy *abuelitos*.

Truth be told, they may have been on to something with the Vicks and its special healing powers. You see, Vicks VapoRub gets its unique scent from a blend of camphor and eucalyptus. These are two powerful plant allies that are known to banish evil and sickness, open roads, and bring in good energies such as healing and angelic beings. Knowing this, we can see that our grandparents may not have been completely crazy after all—all use of Raid aside, of course.

Infusing Vicks for Sickness

Vicks contains some powerful plant oils in it, but mostly it's petroleum jelly, which means it doesn't have much "spirit." To fix this, infuse your Vicks with herbs to enhance its natural powers and make it more magical. Believe it or not, a *curandera* showed me how to do this. It doesn't take very long, but you need to be very present and aware while doing it because Vicks is flammable. Begin by opening a new jar of Vicks and scooping it out into a small mason jar. Bring a small saucepan with a couple inches of water to simmer and put the jar in the hot water. Over low heat, melt the Vicks to a liquid state. While it's melting, put a pinch or two of healing herbs—such as eucalyptus, camphor, rosemary, heal-all, angelica, or hyssop—into a shallow dish. Use whatever you have on hand; just a small amount will do. Sprinkle with a small amount of holy water and pray over them and ask them to assist you with their healing power. Add the herbs to the melted Vicks and let this infuse over low heat for about fifteen minutes, give or take, then strain it into a heat-safe vessel. Do *not* try and put this back into the Vicks jar unless you let it cool first; it will melt the plastic. Also, please don't rely on this method if you are critically ill. Go to the doctor.

Vicks Candle to Open Roads

Sometimes we can see our goals ahead of us, but the road between seems so treacherous or even impossible to traverse. If you are looking to smooth the road ahead and remove obstacles that might stand between you and your goals, you're looking for a road opener!

You'll need:

> 1 *white candle*
> *Vicks VapoRub*
> 1 *pinch blue vervain and/or* abre camino

To begin, cleanse your white candle and carve a cross into the wax on one side and the words "God opens the road" on the other side. Hold it in your hand and say the *Padre Nuestro* while visualizing the candle shimmering with radiant white light. Holding that image in your mind, continue to pray and ask that your road ahead be cleared of all obstacles, that the road be open and protected as you walk easily through. Apply a small amount—remember Vicks is flammable, so don't get carried away—to the candle, just enough to coat it, and then roll the candle in the herb(s). Most folks say you should use only *abre camino* for road opening. Where I am, it's hard to come by unless you special order it. I have used blue vervain for years to open roads instead, and it has done excellent work! Vervain is also known as "herb of the cross" and is said to have grown at the foot of the cross where Christ was left to die. This herb is very powerful, and I highly recommend it as a substitute when *abre camino* is not available.

Once the candle has been rolled in the herbs, either affix it to a plate or set it in a sturdy candleholder and light it, saying a prayer that your roads be opened. When I do this, I visualize a road made of white light extending out from the candle before me, smoothing out the path to my goals and future. You may speak the *Padre Nuestro* over it again at this time.

Vicks VapoRub to Cleanse a Home

In my years serving as resident demon wrangler for my paranormal investigation team, I have had to get rather creative on more than one occasion when supplies were low. This is when I turn to the ancestors—they knew that sometimes all you have is Vicks VapoRub and the Lord. Camphor and eucalyptus, two of the main ingredients in Vicks, carry a powerful vibration that banishes evil and calls in angelic entities and beings of light. In a pinch, you can use Vicks to assist with cleansing and protecting a home from negative entities.

You'll need:

1 pot boiling water
1 white candle (blessed)
Salt (blessed)
Vicks VapoRub

To begin, make sure the home has been thoroughly cleaned. Trying to spiritually cleanse a messy home is like trying to sterilize a cat box while your pet is still using it. Once the home is clean, open all the doors and windows and begin to boil a pot of water on the stove. Light the white candle and say a prayer for protection. While the water is heating up, take the blessed salt around the home and sprinkle a little in every corner of every room, as well as a little in the very center of every room. If you have any left over, go outside and sprinkle it at the four corners of the home. As you do this, pray that God use the salt to cleanse your home of all evil spirits and energies.

Next take your Vicks and go around to all the doors and windows and make the sign of the cross with it above and on either side of all openings—again, praying that all negativity be driven from the home and that the home be protected against further attack. If you want to be really fancy, you could infuse your Vicks ahead of time (see above) with protective herbs like angelica or rue, but that's not necessary. Once that is done, come back to your pot of water, which should be boiling nicely by now. If you'd like to add protective or anti-evil herbs to this water you can, but again, it's not required if you don't have anything on hand. Take a hefty scoop of Vicks and stir it into the water, allowing the steam to carry the scent up and into the room. If your home is small you can probably just leave it on the stove on low heat to simmer away and fill the home with the powerful scent. If you have a larger house, you may (carefully) remove the pot from the stove and carry it through the home, allowing the steam to work its magic in every room. Reheat and add more Vicks to it as necessary. Once this is done, close up all the doors and windows again, and dispose of the water by pouring a little down each drain in the home.

Vicks VapoRub for Cleansing a Person

After *limpias* are done on a person, it can be helpful to anoint them with Vicks to further empower the cleansing and to protect against any further issues. I would use the Vicks to make a sign of the cross on their forehead, the back of their neck, between their shoulder blades, on the center of their chest, the palms of the hands, and the soles of the feet. This will not only help cast off any remaining evil but also protect them once they leave. Please counsel them to not touch their eyes or sensitive areas while it's still on their hands.

If you are trying to cleanse someone from a distance, you may apply Vicks to a doll made in their image in the same manner. If the doll is small, a single cross made over the front and back should help. I would then place this doll next to a white candle that has been blessed.

Vicks for Psychic Development

Yup! You can use Vicks for that too. In meditation it can be helpful to stimulate energy centers such as your third eye by focusing on them until you feel them tingle. A small dab of Vicks in the center of your forehead where your third eye chakra sits can help facilitate this stimulation, as well as aid with opening and unblocking the chakra with the powerful spirits of camphor and eucalyptus.

Red Ribbon

Second only to Vicks VapoRub is red ribbon or string. This tool came up many times in my interviews, and folks had many creative uses for this simple material. Mostly red ribbon is used to deflect evil of all kinds, but it's also occasionally used for other things like healing and luck.

Red Ribbon for Hands/Wrists

Before doing healing work with the hands or handling objects that may contain bad energies, it's common to wrap red ribbon around the hands or wrists to block the evil from entering through them or coming up the arms into the body. This way, *curanderos* and other spiritual workers may handle the energies of sickness and other negative things while staying protected. Wearing red ribbon around the wrist also protects against *Ojo* and other forms of spiritual attack.

Red Ribbon for Colic/Hiccups

To cure hiccups or colic, especially in babies, red string is placed on the forehead in the shape of the cross.

Red Ribbon for Babies

Babies are particularly susceptible to *Mal de Ojo* because they receive a lot of attention and compliments from folks whenever they are out in public. This is believed to make them hot and cranky and cause things like colic. Due to this it's tradition to tie a red ribbon around their wrist to protect them from this affection. Other charms may be added to the ribbon as well such as the *Ojo de Venado* seed.

Red ribbon may also be tied to the four posts of the crib to protect against bad spells and *brujería* sent against your new infant by jealous family members or people in your community. As always, please be careful leaving anything hanging loose near your baby, especially if they are old enough to move around and get into trouble.

Red Ribbon for Farmers

Red ribbon tied to trees in an orchard or crops in a field will protect them from *brujería*. To double the strength, hang scissors from the ribbon. You may also tie the ribbon to fence posts surrounding crops or livestock. Red ribbon may also be tied to animals or woven into their hair to protect them against bad spells and the *Mal de Ojo* from your neighbors.

Red Ribbon and Plants

Many potted houseplants such as aloe, rue, holy basil, and rosemary are said to protect against evil by sending it back to its source. This is why it's common to find these placed on either side of the front door to the home or in large windows. To enhance the protective power of these plants, it's customary to tie a red ribbon on the stalks.

Scissors

I had heard of scissors being used before I began this book, but didn't know just how many possible applications there were! Scissors are mostly for protection against evil. Their sharp edges and ability to slice things into pieces make them a formidable opponent for all evil sent against you. I like this tool because not only does it block out the bad-intentioned spirit or energy, but actively wounds it as well. Protection that bites means whatever tried to harm you will think twice before trying again.

Scissors to Ward Off Nightmares

The most common use for scissors is to ward off nightmares. Everyone has their own way of doing it, but the idea is that an open pair of scissors is placed somewhere around the person while they sleep. Some place the open scissors under the pillow, others place them under the bed. Some place them on the bedside table, and others tack them to the wall above the bed. I don't recommend that last one—they might fall on you during the night.

Some also say that the open scissors should be placed on top of an open Bible that is under the bed.

Scissors to Protect against Witches

A friend of mine learned this trick from her mother who grew up in Guanajuato. To protect against brujas and their hexes that may try to enter your home, place an open pair of scissors in the windowsill and say this prayer to St. Benedict:

> *San Benito va, San Benito viene, San Benito, agárrame a esa bruja que volando viene.*

This translates to, "Saint Benedict goes, Saint Benedict comes, Saint Benedict, grab me that witch that comes flying."

Scissors for an Eclipse

An interesting one that was told to me by a friend who grew up in Mexico City was that people, especially pregnant women, should wear a pair of open scissors tied to them by a red ribbon during an eclipse for protection. Remember, an eclipse is a liminal time in which all kinds of spirits and things may roam the earth.

Scissors and Red Ribbon

Hanging open scissors from a red ribbon will protect just about anything from brujería and bad spirits. This can be used on people, property, and homes.

Mama Ruda

Ruda (rue) is arguably one of the most powerful plants in the Mexican systems of magic. She is used to protect from all manner of evil and witchcraft. She is also reported to have miraculous healing ability, and her sheer presence is said to drive off sickness. However, certain things should be taken into consideration when using this plant. It's so powerful that it needs to be handled very carefully. Applying it directly to the skin can cause photosensitivity, meaning if you go out into the sun after rubbing it on yourself, it could cause you to blister. Also, remember, if you are pregnant or trying to become pregnant, please do not touch rue. Do not rely on rue in times of severe illness—see a doctor if needed.

Rue for an Earache or Eye Problem

Ruda wrapped around the ear is said to relieve earaches. In the case of an eye infection or sty, a sprig of rue placed behind the ear like a pencil so that it juts out past the afflicted eye is said to cure the issue.

Rue for Headache

Rue rubbed on the head is said to relieve headache. Most folks infuse rue in oil for this purpose and apply it to the head. I'm not sure if that lessens the side effects or not, but many people I spoke to swear by it.

Rue for after a Funeral

After returning from a funeral, people give themselves and their loved ones a *limpia con huevo* and a *barrida* (see the *Limpias* chapter) with rue to remove the bad energies and banish bad spirits that may have attached to them while in the cemetery. Many cultures, including Mexican culture, believe that death has its own energy that needs to be cleaned away after you come in contact with it.

Rue for Breaking Hexes

Rue is a powerful and wise plant. She understands the ins and outs of all spells, and this makes her a formidable spellbreaker.

Added to baths or floor washes, she's known to remove all manner of hexes and curses. Mixed with salt, she may be used as a floor sweep. Placed in the shoes, she protects against evil.

Water Glass Magic

Glasses of water are used heavily throughout American Brujeria. The element of water is an excellent filter that can help us separate and trap negativity while simultaneously refreshing the flow of blessings and good energy. Most folks prefer to use a fancy goblet or wineglass for this work, but any glass vessel will work. Once these glasses are used for this work, though, they are no longer for drinking—especially those that have been used as a filter for negativity. You should clean them after each use—with soap and white vinegar—but they should be considered contaminated and employed only for filtration from then on.

Camphor Water

You may buy blocks of camphor online and at some botanicas and hardware stores. These are used mundanely as an alternative to mothballs or a way to keep your tools and silverware from tarnishing. Spiritually, camphor lifts and opens the energy of a place. This makes it ideal for opening roads, opening the mind, and driving out evil spirits. In fact, a block of camphor placed on a charcoal disk creates an extremely powerful smoke that drives out all evil spirits from a home. Don't breathe it in, though—it's very intense!

To filter out the bad energy in your home, fill a glass with water and place one block of camphor in the water. Let it sit in a prominent place for several days. I like to do this after I've cleaned my home to continue to keep the good energy long after the work is done. After about a week, dispose of the water—flushing is best—and begin with new materials. A lot of folks like to place this glass behind their front door to filter out any energy coming into the home. I have pets and a clumsy husband, so I set it on my mantel. You may also opt to set it on your front porch beside your door or in a window as you see fit.

Blue Water

Blue water is simple to make and excellent for psychic protection and to safeguard against *Mal de Ojo*. Glasses of blue water are generally used as a filter and set out during psychic readings. They may also be placed in windowsills or prominent places in the home to absorb and trap *Mal de Ojo*.

To make blue water you'll want to combine pure, blessed water in a glass with laundry bluing. I prefer to use the Mrs. Stewart's brand you can find in most grocery stores. It's nontoxic and comes in a liquid form. You may also use "Anil" balls that you can purchase at most botanicas. Either way, add as much bluing as you would like. I prefer mine rather dark, but it's up to you. Place the glass wherever it is needed the most, whether that's on the table where you will be doing psychic readings or in a window facing your nosy neighbor.

Alum Water

Alum or *alumbre* is a curious substance used heavily in American folk magic. Given its ability to tighten skin and its incredibly sour taste, it is often used to shut something down—particularly lies and gossip. It also absorbs water and other fluids rather quickly and may be placed around the home to "dry out" spirits and ghosts, causing them to weaken or flee. Its absorbent qualities and affinity for binding gossip also make it an excellent choice for cleansing yourself of negative talk. Simply rub it down your body from head to toe, then burn it on a charcoal disk outdoors. But we're here to talk about *alum water*.

When added to a glass of water, alum brings light! That's especially true for a glass of water that is given to your spirits. I will make this when I want to honor them in a special way. However, if I want to bring illumination or clarity to my home, I will place a glass of water with a small chunk of alum in it somewhere prominent like on the mantel. This will help bring forth the truth and give peace and illumination to the home. It's often handy to have on a table for psychic readings to bring clarity. I often recommend praying to St. Lucy or St. Claire when making or using alum water.

Reversal Water

Water is good at many things, including trapping and purifying negativity. It also has a unique ability to listen to our needs and respond accordingly. To make a ward that will trap and reverse evil, negativity, and *Mal de Ojo*, you'll need a glass of water, a small plate, salt, and one small white candle.

To begin, bless the water, candle, and the salt by praying the *Padre Nuestro* or *Dios te Salve* over them. Fill the glass with the water and add three pinches of the salt to it in the name of the Holy Trinity. Then speak to the water and ask that it trap all evil spirits, all bad magic, and all bad energy. Furthermore, ask that it reverse the negativity and send it back to where it came from! When you are done, set the plate on top of the glass and hold them together firmly as you flip them both upside down. If some water comes out, don't worry—just wipe it up and continue. Place the white candle on top of the upside down glass and light it while saying a prayer. When the candle is finished burning, you are ready. Set the glass in a window or near a door to protect your home and family. Dispose of the water and start over once a week.

Garlic, Horseshoes, *y* Más!

Now let's look at all the other items and rituals I've found beneficial or protective in everyday use through my studies. This section is fun and easy and might give you inspiration to employ things you may have lying around the house already.

Ajo

Ajo, or garlic, is a powerful plant used in Mexican magic. It is excellent for driving out bad spirits, bad energy, and sickness —reflected in its medicinal ability to kill bacteria and other illness-causing microbes when taken internally or applied to a surface. It is also considered to be sacred to St. Michael (San Miguel), defeater of all evil. Other stories say that it was placed or grew at the foot of the cross of Jesus to keep the devil at bay while he was at his most vulnerable.

Placed by the door, it prevents sickness and bad spirits from entering. It may also be hung from red string for this purpose or tied to the doorknob with a red string. Garlic worn about the neck on a red cord will prevent illness.

Cutting open a clove of garlic will expose its inner juices. Using this open side of the clove, you may mark your doorways and property with the sign of the cross to protect against bad spirits and illness. Burning garlic skins exorcises evil spirits.

Horseshoes

Horseshoes or other things made of iron have long been used as protection against bad spirits and misfortune. A horseshoe hung above the front door protects against all manner of evil and helps bring luck into the home. There's some debate on the proper way to display them though. Some say you should have the tips pointing up so that it holds all your luck. Others say they should point down so that luck rains down on all those who enter the home. Use your best judgment.

Horseshoes hung from red ribbon are protective, and you can find garlic braided with red ribbon with horseshoes hanging from the bottom to hang in the home. These are extremely protective and show the similarities between Italian and Mexican folk magic. Spain and Italy are quite close, after all.

Amuletos

Amuletos are simple protection charms that can really come in handy. To create one, take a small bit of red fabric and sew it into a square, making sure that one edge remains open. Stuff the small square with protective herbs such as rue, angelica, devil's shoestring, garlic, etc. Some say you should add a bit of yourself—hair, nails, etc.—to the *amuleto*, but I don't like to leave my personal concerns out in the open. Many folks also like to incorporate an image of a beloved saint either slipped inside or sewn on the outside of the charm. Say a prayer as you sew it shut the rest of the way and then pin it somewhere under your clothing where it won't be seen. I feed my *amuletos* a protection oil once a month by simply putting a drop on my finger and rubbing it into the fabric while I say the St. Michael Prayer. You may use the *Padre Nuestro* or the *Dios te Salve* instead if you like.

Night Protection

A lot of superstition surrounds the act of sleeping in cultures around the world, and Mexico is no different. Many things can be employed to protect yourself while you sleep, and most of them are extremely simple and easy to use.

Apples come up surprisingly often. It's said that if you place an apple on your bedside table, it will absorb all the bad energy that might come for you in the night. The apple should be thrown out and replaced every three days or so. Don't eat an apple after it's been used for this.

Glasses of water placed on a nightstand or under the bed also hold significance. It's said that placing a glass of water beside you while you sleep will act as a filter and trap all the bad energy coming to you in the night, much like the apple. However, you should not drink the water in the morning, because it's full of the bad energy. Some even believe that the bubbles that form on the side of the glass in the night are the trapped negativity. Some say it should be a glass of salt water—which would be a helpful deterrent from accidentally drinking it in the middle of the night.

Holy water placed in little bottles on the headboard, nightstand, or under the bed is said to protect against all sorts of night attacks.

In Mexican culture it is believed that we leave our bodies at night and travel through mirrors. In some places it is customary to cover the mirrors at night to prevent your spirit from slipping away and getting lost.

House Protection

Small bottles of holy water may be placed above the doors, under beds, and in windowsills to protect from all manner of evil and bring blessings into the home. Holy water is especially useful when it comes to banishing demons and evil spirits.

On Palm Sunday, blessed palms are passed out at church. It's customary to make them into the shape of a cross during mass and then take them home with you. The crosses can be displayed above doors or in windows as powerful forms of protection. I've also watched *abuelitas* weave them into baskets, mats, and more!

The front door of the home may be washed with a special brew to reinforce the protective boundary. Steep protective herbs like rue and garlic in hot water and let rest until the liquid is cool enough to handle. Then, using a rag, wash the door and doorframe. This protects the home and keeps evil from entering.

Las Chanclas

Something that came up a couple of times in my research is sandals. If you grew up Latinx, you undoubtedly were threatened with *la chancla* at least once in your life, since sandals or slippers are favorite spanking tools for unruly children in our culture. I was surprised when they showed up again as a way to ward off evil. Several people recalled their elders placing their sandals by the door in the sign of the cross—with one placed over the other. I guess even the devil is afraid of *la chancla*.

An Old Boot

I also ran across a staggering number of magical uses for old boots or shoes. I think this must be a carryover from Europe, where they are frequently used for protection and fertility.

Old boots are often placed outside the front door or in walls as a sort of decoy charm. The worn boots carry the scent of a human, which attracts negative spirits looking for someone to harm. Once they go inside the boot, it's said that they are unable to get out because they can't move in reverse. There is a lot of lore surrounding evil spirits and their mobility—lots of strange ideas like they can only move in straight lines or can't back up. Others say they have to compulsively count things, which is why placing jars of sand, rice, or beans by the front door is protective. The spirit is forced to count them before they can enter the home, and they are usually considered bad at counting and have to start over again and again and are either destroyed by the sun or stuck there forever counting, depending on the version of the story told. It's also said that a saint named John Schorne cast the devil into a boot and trapped him there, which might lend some authority to the use of old boots.

I was also told on one occasion that there was a *curandero* using an old boot for *limpias* when times were tough and there was no money for herbs, eggs, or other tools. This goes along with the idea that bad things may be trapped inside them.

On another occasion I was told a really interesting story about someone's *abuelo* who had a habit of astral projecting in his sleep and walking the perimeter of the home to protect it during the night. When his daughter left home, he gave her one of his old boots and asked her to put it on her porch—that way when he was astral projecting at night, he could find her and keep her safe.

Ghosts

When faced with ghosts, it's easy to be overwhelmed and terrified. Mexican people are no strangers to ghosts and deal with them on a regular basis. As I was researching this book, folks seemed to favor one of two ways to banish ghosts. The first is praying the *Padre Nuestro*—this is the most common go-to in this situation—or the *Dios te Salve*. However, if that doesn't seem to work, there is an alternative. Profusely swearing with as much force as you can muster is also said to drive out ghosts and evil spirits. I recommend attempting these only if the ghost seems to be of evil intent. If it seems benign, ask it what it needs and see if you can help. Ghosts can be handy to have as allies.

If you find yourself suffering from sleep paralysis, it's often believed to be caused by ghosts. Making the sign of the cross with your tongue, either in the air or on the roof of your mouth, is said to release the paralysis, as does praying the *Padre Nuestro* in your head. However, if you find yourself suffering from chronic sleep paralysis, this might mean you are a natural astral projector. Many people I know who are really adept at astral projection used to suffer from sleep paralysis nearly every night, but it stopped once they began projecting on a regular basis. You see, sleep paralysis leaves your body asleep but your mind awake, which is the ideal state for leaving your body. The trouble is that, if you're not expecting it, this paralysis can be terrifying and most folks naturally panic instead of seeing it as an opportunity for exploration.

Combat Magic

In our culture, spiritual warfare is something that happens frequently. We have learned effective ways to deal with our enemies or people who cross us by throwing hexes. This is common with oppressed people: we have to find ways to fight in secret. This means that you may very quickly find yourself the target of a nasty bruja's wrath. So what do you do? Below are four spells that come in handy for dealing with these problems.

St. Michael Protection Spell
Sometimes we know that we will be heading into danger or going through a perilous time. In these instances it's best to set up some form of protection for ourselves. Who better to protect us than the mightiest of all archangels? It's time to call on St. Michael.

You'll need:

2 St. Michael prayer cards
1 strand of hair (from the person you are protecting)
Red thread
1 sewing needle
1 red candle or a St. Michael novena

To begin, take one of the St. Michael prayer cards and lay it facedown on the table before you. Place the strand of hair on top of the card—folded if it's long so that it's within the borders of the card. It sometimes helps to tape the hair in place just to make sure it stays put. Take the other card and place it on top, faceup. This way the hair is sandwiched between two St. Michael prayer cards that are back-to-back with their fronts with the image of Michael facing outward.

Next, take the red thread and needle, and begin to sew the cards together along the edges. As you do this, continually pray to St. Michael for protection with words from the heart, the St. Michael Prayer, or both. When the packet is finished being sewn together, hold it between your palms and pray again for protection. Keep this packet, and every time you need protection, burn a candle on top of it. I prefer to use a St. Michael novena because it's the safest way to do so. I know others who like to use tea lights. Use whatever is best for your situation.

Salt Water Cleanse

Use this to cleanse away *mal brujería* and evil spirits from the home.
You'll need:

1 white candle dressed with Fiery Wall or Cast Off Evil oil
Incense
1 saint card of your choosing (If in doubt, use Jesus or St. Michael.)

1 glass bowl

Water (Holy water, spring water, or moon water is preferable but not required.)

Blessed sea salt

1 pair of scissors

This spell is best done on a Saturday or Sunday during a waning moon, but can still be performed at any time. To begin, open all windows, doors, closets, and cupboards. Then light the white candle and incense, and say a prayer to St. Michael for protection. Set the saint card flat on the table and place the glass bowl on top of it. Fill the bowl with water and add three scoops of sea salt in the name of the Father, Son, and Holy Spirit. Stir the water counterclockwise until the salt completely dissolves. Open the scissors and place them on top of the bowl making an X with the points up—if you don't have scissors, you can use two sharp knives. Make the sign of the cross over the bowl and scissors three times, blessing it in the name of the Father, Son, and Holy Spirit, then pray the following:

> *May this blessed creature of water wash away all darkness and sin. May this blessed creature of salt send all evil creatures to flight. May these blessed scissors cut through the tricks of the enemy and bar them from returning. Amen.*

Remove the scissors from the top of the bowl and set them aside. Take the bowl around the house, dipping your hand into the water and flicking the water drops all over. Some folks like to use bundles of herbs like rosemary or rue to sprinkle the water; it's up to you. Pay special attention to the floors, walls, closet spaces, and thresholds (windowsills and doorways). Pray the whole time that God or beings of light enter your home and make it safe and holy once more. When you are done, close everything back up and let the candle burn out all the way. The scissors may be put away in their normal spot or placed above the door or in the window to protect the home.

Reversal Spell

Reversal spells are used to remove and send back evil magic and energy. For this you'll want to use a Double Reversal or Reversible candle, which generally come in three varieties: white and black, red and black, or green and black. The red is for love problems, the green is for money problems, and the white is all-purpose.

You'll need:

A small mirror
Holy water or Florida Water
1 Double Reversal novena candle
Reversal oil
Agrimony
Rue
Garlic
Red pepper flakes

Begin by cleansing the mirror with holy water or Florida Water. Then take your cleansed novena candle and hold it upside down in your hand so that the black half is upward. Take a moment to tune in to the feeling of the hex or crossed condition and bring it to the surface. Rub yourself downward with the black end of the novena in the same manner you'd do the *limpia con huevo* to pull off the hex. Dress the candle in your usual fashion with the reversal oil, agrimony and rue (to remove and reverse the hex), the garlic (to exorcise evil), and the red pepper flakes (to add extra kick to the reversal). Burn the novena on the mirror to send the hex back to the one who sent it.

Hexing Spell

I don't like giving out hexes and other evil spells, but sometimes you must defend yourself. Use this sparingly and only when you really have to.

You'll need:

1 hot pepper (your choice how brutal to be; you might want to wear gloves)
Knife
1 picture of the person you are hexing
Something to write with
1 black candle dressed with Black Arts or D.U.M.E oil
Black pepper
Black mustard seeds
Red pepper flakes
Needle and thread
9 pins or needles
Jar
Vinegar
5 pennies (optional)

This is best done on a Saturday during a waning or dark moon. Cut the top off the pepper and carefully scoop out the inside. Across the photo write exactly what you want the person to do—such as "Leave me alone" or "Have bad luck!" until the photo is completely covered with writing. Anoint the photo in all four corners and the center with whatever oil you used on the candle. Fold it away from you until it's small enough to stuff into the pepper, and fill the rest of the way with the black pepper (to repel), black mustard seeds (for confusion), and red pepper flakes (to inflame). Once it's filled up, sew the top of the pepper closed. You may also wish to drip the black candle wax around the seam to further secure it. Once this is done, stab all nine pins into the pepper with intentional fury. When you are done, you have two options. If you're mad, stuff it into a small jar and pour vinegar over it then seal it up. You can then place this somewhere gross like under the sink or behind the toilet. On the other hand, if you're *really* mad, take it to a crossroads and leave it there with five pennies. Don't look back.

9

Los Antepasados

One of my main goals for this book is to connect people to their ancestors by bringing back the traditions and magic of our people. So what better way to connect with our ancestors than through veneration and working with them in our daily spiritual practices? We as Mexican American people know that they never truly leave us, and death is a celebrated part of our culture. In this chapter we will cover the basics of working with our beloved dead and how we can incorporate them into our daily lives once more.

Building an Ancestor Altar

Building an ancestor altar is very simple and doesn't have to take up much space. Much like when we make a saint altar, we want to be sure that the area is clean both physically and spiritually. After that, though, the construction is largely up to you, so feel free to be creative! Some common things that are placed on the altar are photos of the deceased; items that belonged to them such as rosaries, Bibles, or jewelry; things that they enjoyed in life like favorite cigarettes, favorite liquor, or favorite perfume; as well as items for spiritual maintenance such as holy water or Florida Water. These last two can be used to clean and bless the altar as necessary. I also like to have a Bible near, if not on, the altar so that I can perform bibliomancy when asking for guidance.

The other things you'll want on the altar are a white candle, a glass of water, and incense. These are used in much the same way as we've described in previous chapters. The candle acts as a beacon for your ancestors. The water is an offering and a conduit their energy. The incense helps elevate them and carries our prayers up to heaven. These things together allow us to facilitate the connection between ourselves and their spirits. In order to maintain a strong connection, be sure to keep your altar clean both physically and energetically so it remains a pure conduit for their spirits. Dirty altars are not pleasant for them to inhabit, and they're likely to leave. They also attract negative spirits that may try to harm us.

Taboos

Certain things are considered taboo or forbidden when it comes to the ancestor altar, and they are important to discuss. The first is that photos of the living should not be placed on the ancestor altar. This is said to bring the living person a speedy death.

The second most common taboo is placing ancestor altars in the bedroom. Our bedroom is where we often get naked and engage in sexual activities that the family does not really want to watch. Plus, many folks who have loud or intrusive families find it difficult to sleep when their ancestors are in their room at night. This issue can be complicated because sometimes we don't have room anywhere else or we live in a studio apartment where our bedroom is our whole house. What do we do then? First, you may wish to cover your ancestor altar with a sheet at night before you go to bed or before any nudity or sexual activities. You may also put up a partition screen or a room divider to create a separate space between the ancestors and the rest of the room.

Some folks also say that you should not let salt anywhere near your ancestor altar as it chases away the dead. They often go so far as to say that any food you offer them should not contain any salt. I don't feel this way about the food: the ancestors deserve flavor. Also, we need to remember that a popular *Día de los Muertos* tradition says to put a dish of salt on the *ofrenda* (offering) to keep bad spirits at bay. I think where people get confused is that earthbound spirits (those who haven't crossed over) can be troublesome and are repelled by earthly things like salt. However, the ancestors that we are working with have crossed over and are no longer susceptible to such trivial things. Others also say that burning cleansing herbs will chase them away, but I've also found this to be a myth for the same reasons. In fact, I always burn cleansing herbs before calling them forth as I find it helps them come through more clearly with less interference.

Working with the Ancestors

Once your altar is set up, you may begin working with the ancestors. If you are the first in your family to do this, they may be a little sleepy or in need of maintenance. Either way, be sure to spend some time lighting novenas, feeding them, and saying prayers before you begin to ask for favors. This introductory period should last at least a month, after which you may begin to make requests.

Your ancestors are the number one spirits invested in your growth and well-being. They, more than anyone, want to help you, and you need them as well. Whenever you have a problem, who do you go to first? Your family! When you are happy, who do you call first? Your family! Just because they have died doesn't mean they no longer care. In fact, in death many of them are much more able to help you than when they were alive! So feel free to let your ancestors know about your life—what you are working on, what you are proud of. Let them know when you are scared and need their protection or when you need their guidance. Tell them when you are short on rent and ask if they can help. Burn candles to them when you ask, and say prayers for them.

Calling the Ancestors

Our ancestors are around us all the time, whether we've called them forth or not. However, the act of calling them forth really pulls them further into our world and helps them to interact with us. This process is simple. You light your ancestor candle and speak aloud something along the lines of "I call forth my ancestors, those who have found God on the other side and wish to guide and protect me in this lifetime. May they be here with me now, and all the days of my life." This does two things: First, it gives them permission to come forward and interact with us. Second, it specifies who exactly it is we are talking to. It can get dicey if we don't express exactly who we are speaking to on the other side. If we don't specify, just about anything can answer. So make sure to call forth the ancestors that are here for your "highest good." When you're done, thank them and extinguish the candle to close the session.

Praying for the Dead

One of the most important things that we can do for our ancestors is pray for them. We all have a good chunk of ancestors who have made it to the Promised Land and are happily watching over us. However, there are also many ancestors that might not have gotten there for one reason or another. Sometimes spirits get lost or stuck on their way to the light. Sometimes they hold on to their anger, addictions, or fear, and it holds them back from joining God. Some are being punished for their evil deeds. No matter the reason, our prayers can help them heal and find their way back to God.

The most common way to pray for the ancestors is to pray the rosary for all the souls trapped in purgatory. You may or may not believe in purgatory, but the metaphor remains relevant for attempting to help those who have been trapped on the other side. This includes but is not limited to our ancestors. You may also pray words from the heart, and I often go through a short list that isn't always the same but goes something like this, "I pray for my ancestors who have not made it to God. If they are lost, let them be found. If they are scared, may they be brave. If they are damned, may they find deliverance. If they are stuck, may they be released. If they are wounded, may they be healed. If they are ready, may they find the light. If they are sorry, may they be forgiven." And so on and so forth.

Feeding the Ancestors

Feeding your ancestors is important! It's what sustains them, strengthens them, and helps anchor them in our world. I recommend feeding them at least once a week, if not more. This is done simply by calling them forth, placing a plate of food on their altar, and saying some prayers for them. You may also eat at the ancestor altar on special occasions—sharing a meal is a great way to connect with family! They also enjoy beverages such as coffee, liquor, and soda.

Elevating the Ancestors

Ancestor elevation works on a theory that the better standing our ancestors have in heaven, the better position they'll be in to watch over us, guide us, and protect us. It is believed that through certain rituals we may be able to elevate the ancestors to new heights and therefore benefit ourselves here on earth.

You'll need:

9 *thick books or bricks*
1 *white cloth*
1 *white novena candle*
1 *glass of water*

Begin on the first day by placing the first book or brick on your ancestor altar and covering it with the white cloth. On top of the cloth place the lit white candle and the glass of water. Say prayers for the elevation of your ancestors. Pray that anything holding them back—regret, fear, their sins, etc.—be removed so that they may ascend higher. As you do this, imagine your prayers lifting them up higher and higher. Do this every day for nine days, adding a book or a brick each day. Eventually you'll have a small tower! At the end of the nine days, remove the bricks or books and store them away. You can repeat this as many times or as often as you would like.

Common Questions

Who counts as an ancestor?
There are many types of ancestors, including those in your bloodline going all the way back to the very first people. There are also our loved ones and friends who have passed on that we are not related to—these still count. Also there are ancestors of our trade. For instance, if you are a writer, the writers who came before are your ancestors as well. Basically anyone who has died that has a connection to you in some way can be an ancestor, depending on

how you approach it. I have also known people who create ancestor altars for their pets that have passed on.

What if I don't know who my ancestors are?
This is fine too! You just pray to them as a unit, and they will hear you. I also highly recommend getting acquainted with online resources for genealogy research. It's fascinating, and with modern technology it's easier now than it ever has been to find out where we came from. Also if you have any living relatives, ask them for stories about your family, their parents and grandparents, etc. It's a great place to start.

What about my ancestors that were problematic?
(Abusers, addicts, racists, etc.)
We all have jerks in our family tree. You can choose not to work with these ancestors; it's largely up to you. I do find sometimes, though, that some of these problematic ancestors have found healing on the other side and wish to make up for their misdeeds in life by acting as guides and helpers for us now. It's up to you whether or not you accept that help, but you should say prayers for them either way as it will contribute to their healing and yours as well. If they are acting up or becoming a menace, ask that your good ancestors deal with them on your behalf. They're usually more than happy to.

I'm adopted. Who do I pray to? My birth family?
Or my adopted family?
Both! They might each wish to help guide and protect you in this life, or you may find that one line wants to work with you more or less than the other. Take some time to feel it out, and go with what is most comfortable for you.

A Prayer for the Liminal

O Heavenly Mother, she who conceived without sin, our
most glorious Virgin Guadalupe, we call to you and ask
your intercession. May we tear down the wall and heal
the wounds of colonization.

May we be brought together through the power of the
liminal people, those who are caught in between. May
they form a bridge that helps us heal each other and the
holy spirits above.

May we learn to love and accept ourselves as valid Mexican
American people who have a purpose in this world. We
have gente and we are not alone. Open our eyes to this
miracle so that we may find each other.

May we reject all borders and embrace the suffering of our
people. May those of us with privilege help those of us
without. May we share our opportunities and stand up
for our people. Open our arms so we may embrace each
other.

May we hear the voices of our ancestors, and may they
guide us back to our magic. The spells and breath of our
people are powerful, and it's through these secrets that
we may reclaim what was lost. Open our ears to hear
their wisdom.

May those who are lost find their way back to us. Those who think they are too black or too white to be Latinx are our brothers and sisters and deserve to be embraced in our world. We pray that they find their place and uphold the colorful voices of our people.

May our culture be healed of its racism, homophobia, and other injustices brought to us by our colonizers. A new era is dawning, and our hearts are open to all of our people.

May we bless the liminal and recognize the sacredness of their role as mediators.

Amen.

Bibliography/ Recommended Reading

Arredondo, Alexis A., and Eric J. Labrado. *Magia Magia*. Mobile, AL: Conjure South Publications, 2020.

Avila, Elena, and Joy Parker. *Woman Who Glows in the Dark*. New York: Tarcher, 2000.

Buenaflor, Erika. *Cleansing Rites of Curanderismo*. Rochester, VT: Bear and Company, 2018.

Curandera, Curious. *Curious Curandera*, 9AD, *curiouscurandera. blogspot.com/*.

Madsen, William, and Claudia Madsen. *A Guide to Mexican Witchcraft*. Mexico: Editorial Minutiae, 1974.

Malbrough, Ray T. *The Magical Power of the Saints*. Woodbury, MN: Llewellyn Worldwide, 2014.

Valeriano, Antonio. *Nican Mopohua*, 1989, *springfieldop.org*.

About the Author

J. Allen Cross is a practicing witch of Mexican, Native American, and European descent, whose craft was shaped by his Catholic upbringing and mixed family culture. Living in his home state of Oregon, he works as a psychic medium and occult specialist for a well-known paranormal investigation team out of the Portland metro area. When he's not investigating, he enjoys providing spells and potions to his local community, exploring haunted and abandoned places, consulting for other workers and investigators, and, of course, writing about witchcraft and folk magic. Follow him on Instagram at @oregon_wood_witch.

To Our Readers

Weiser Books, an imprint of Red Wheel/Weiser, publishes books across the entire spectrum of occult, esoteric, speculative, and New Age subjects. Our mission is to publish quality books that will make a difference in people's lives without advocating any one particular path or field of study. We value the integrity, originality, and depth of knowledge of our authors.

Our readers are our most important resource, and we appreciate your input, suggestions, and ideas about what you would like to see published.

Visit our website at *www.redwheelweiser.com* to learn about our upcoming books and free downloads, and be sure to go to *www.redwheelweiser.com/newsletter* to sign up for newsletters and exclusive offers.

You can also contact us at *info@rwwbooks.com* or at

Red Wheel/Weiser, LLC
65 Parker Street, Suite 7
Newburyport, MA 01950